MW01620206

We Are All Born Entrepreneurs

We Are All Born Entrepreneurs

Steve Welch

HC ISBN 978-0-557-29709-2

To My Parents

Thank you for providing me love and support while at the same time the confidence to learn and grow.

To My Wife

Thank you for loving me and allowing me to be myself.

To My Children

Thank you for providing me with a joy I could not have imagined before you were here.

Contents

Preface

Time should be one of the most precious elements in our lives. I always have asked those around me to respect my time, and I promise to do the same for you. Therefore, this book is deliberately concise; I know you are anxious to learn how to ignite your entrepreneurial zeal, so let's get right to it.

Why am I qualified to serve as an entrepreneurial guide? In less than seven years, I built a biotech manufacturing business with almost zero capital, and then, at the age of twenty-nine, sold it to a Fortune 500 company. During the time when I was busy launching and shaping the company, I never understood the uniqueness of this accomplishment at such a young age. It was not until a few years later, when I was able to reflect on the unusual path my life had taken, that I digested the impact of my journey.

Although the ideas in this book highlight my experiences in a technology start-up and the journeys of other entrepreneurs, the lessons from those experiences can be applied to almost every independent-minded thinker in the business world. These stories resonate whether you are an aspiring entrepreneur, already immersed in entrepreneurial ventures, an entrepreneur embedded in a large organization, or someone who enjoys an American dream-come-true story.

The word *entrepreneur* elicits different visions from everyone. To some, the word conjures up an image of a crazy uncle who invents thingamajigs, while others envision a neighbor who launched his or her own local restaurant or a self-employed aunt who is a freelance graphics designer for nonprofit organizations. To others, the ultimate entrepreneur is twenty-year-old Bill Gates taking on the conventional wisdom of IBM. These manifestations are all accurate because entrepreneurs are everywhere, making big and small changes, looking at the way the world works, and concluding: "I can make it work *better*."

Entrepreneurship is in our DNA. Need proof? Take a minute to watch a two-year-old child. You will see a fearless person trying to make the world work more efficiently. Children are in continual pursuit of knowledge and new challenges. They are constantly expanding their limits and always seeking a better understanding of the world around them.

Since the earliest humans walked the earth, those with entrepreneurial skills have possessed significant survival advantages. Those that experimented with new means of hunting ultimately found better solutions, leading them to live longer than their more complacent neighbors. Thus, entrepreneurship has been passed down and embedded in our DNA.

In the past decade, I have seen that DNA exemplified by hundreds of successful entrepreneurs. While each of these individuals is unique, there are some common traits among them. The main characteristic is that they are passionate lifetime learners who constantly search for means to improve the world. They possess a willingness and desire to be accountable for their successes and failures. And they have positive personalities. They look at a problem and see opportunity.

So where do entrepreneurs operate? Basically, everywhere! Some entrepreneurs are self-employed, and some work at small start-ups. Some build their own businesses, while others work in large organizations, helping their company propel forward. No matter how they go about their entrepreneurial endeavors, without these innovative thinkers willing to take action, we might still be hunters and gatherers, chasing after our dinner while carrying our children on our backs.

If Johann Gutenberg had not developed the printing press in the fifteenth century, the world might never have known the democratic and capitalistic systems of Thomas Paine and Adam Smith that were spread through the printed word. If Edison had not considered each of his two thousand failures a learning experience before he invented the modern-day lightbulb, we might still be using candles to read at night. In 1928, if Alexander Fleming had not questioned why all the bacteria on his plate were killed by a type of mold, the world would be without penicillin, and many of us would have lost friends and family. These are some extreme examples of the importance of entrepreneurs in our society, but they demonstrate a key point: without entrepreneurs, society would stand still. Their constant challenging of the norm is what creates change and innovation and leads to job growth and opportunities in our society.

For these reasons, it is critical that we find ways to bring out the entrepreneurial spirit that is alive in all of us.

I hope that the stories in this book, as well as the missteps and solutions that I and other successful entrepreneurs learned along the way, help you unlock *your* inner entrepreneur.

Acknowledgments

A special thank you to Diane Bones, Jack Welch, and Katie Sweeney for helping in the editing process …

And the hundreds of entrepreneurs that afforded me the time to discuss their ventures. I heard more interesting and exciting stories then I could possible include in this book. I am grateful for every minute and enriched by every encounter. . .

And to David Speers for managing the publishing of this book.

One

The End

I would like to open my story by telling you how it ends.

At 1:10 p.m. on July 2, 2007, Steve Kleepak hung up his cell phone, raised his hand to shake mine, looked me in the eye, and proclaimed: "Welcome to Parker, Steve."

Mr. Kleepak, vice president of operations at Parker Hannifin Corporation, was obviously elated about the call that officially confirmed Parker's acquisition of my company, Mitos Technologies, Inc. The deal was closed.

In Mr. Kleepak's mind, the purchase allowed Parker to penetrate a new market that his company had struggled to enter for years, with access to a new crop of customers that valued the products offered by this global corporation. Mr. Kleepak was clearly thrilled with his accomplishment.

As the sole owner of Mitos, I was also overjoyed at the completion of the sale. But as I reached out to shake Mr. Kleepak's hand, I was also overcome with emotion. While Mr. Kleepak had just purchased a company, I had just sold the last six and a half years of my life's work. I had put my blood, sweat, and tears into the business, both figuratively and literally. The company that—as of this moment—was now Parker's had enabled me to make enduring friendships and provided me with a self-confidence that I don't think I could have otherwise gained. Building my business challenged me mentally, physically, and emotionally, and changed who I was in ways that I could never have predicted.

So it is no surprise that I was internally conflicted as Mr.Kleepak and I shook hands on the deal. My smile was genuine, if a bit confused. I probably looked like a father escorting his daughter down the aisle on her wedding day: happy for the grown child that he so dearly loves and has nurtured through the years, yet overcome by intense feelings as he watches his "baby" begin her new life without him. Basically, the completion of the sale and that simple handshake symbolized a tsunami of sentiments. Rising like a tidal wave among the other intense feelings, however, was the comprehension that one significant, almost unbelievable, chapter in my life had ended while a new one was about to begin.

A few minutes after Mr. Kleepak and I exchanged hearty congratulations, my six-person Mitos leadership group joined me and the rest of the Parker team for a celebratory lunch. It was an odd mix. The Parker team consisted mostly of Caucasian males with an average age of about fifty. As the team from Parker introduced themselves, it was my right-hand man Charles Meadows who realized that our Mitos group had a median age of twenty-nine and that our combined individual years in business did not equal the amount of time that Mr. Kleepak had worked for Parker. As my young, diverse team sat at the table, I realized—perhaps for the first time—the uniqueness of our accomplishment. Our team had built a business that would live on beyond us. After the sale, Mitos would have a new name, but the innovations, products, and services that our group of twenty-somethings had built would continue to be of value to society, with or without us. That was a truly humbling and fulfilling realization for all of us. Yes, we were young—I wasn't even 30 yet—but we had used our youthful energy and enthusiasm to forge a company that manufactured a variety of products designed to benefit people. Our efforts had lowered the costs and helped increase the availability of biotech drugs and vaccines throughout the world. Our products assisted in the manufacturing of everything from the flu vaccine to the newest cancer drugs.

Midway through lunch, my BlackBerry vibrated. A text from my wife confirmed that the funds from the sale had been wired from Parker's bank account into ours. Now a totally new emotion overwhelmed me, and, as I stared down at my phone and focused on the stunning text message, I actually felt sick to my stomach. The price of my business wasn't a secret, of course. A month ago, we had settled on a sale agreement, but it was quite another matter to actually *see* the amount of money that had been transferred into our bank account. So while I was prepared for this transaction, it was impossible to truly absorb the impact of the event until it had actually happened. It was at that precise moment when I *fully* understood that, at the age of twenty-nine, I had earned a lifetime of financial security for myself and my family.

What made this fact even more difficult to digest was that, only six and a half years earlier, I had been trying to figure out how to start this same business out of my six-hundred-square-foot apartment, with my bedroom doubling as my office.

In the Beginning

It all began with an idea I had for a new product for the biotech field. I was always somewhat entrepreneurial at heart, but at age twenty-three, I was especially inspired because I believed that my idea might, if you'll pardon the cliché, change the world. In addition, the product I envisioned producing was in a growing market—the biotech industry—that was hungry for innovations and efficiency. And all of this happened at a stage in my life when I had nothing to lose were I to take a chance on my business idea; I didn't have a wife or children who would suffer if my idea bombed. But there was a hitch—isn't there *always?* I was a college graduate, yet I never took a business class in my life. And I basically had no money to start the business. Plus, descending from a long line of corporate types and teachers, I never knew anyone who had started a technology business from scratch. I did not realize that angels investors or venture capitalists existed. I barely knew what the word *entrepreneur* meant.

Despite these roadblocks, I chose to quit my full-time job and move ahead with my idea. My inexperience was apparent as I went to various banks to try to borrow money to start the business. I quickly learned that banks do not lend money to twenty-four-year-olds with no capital or other assets. I had no idea what I was in for.

To say it was a difficult road would be a total understatement. How tough was it to launch and build my dream? Sometimes, I think I have blocked out some of the most grueling challenges. But I definitely remember that it was not uncommon for me to work hundred-hour weeks during the first three years of starting my company. Actually, because my mind was never able to leave the business, I was *always* working. So much for a bustling social life or romance for the struggling entrepreneur …

But don't cry for me. Eventually, I found and fell in love with a fantastic woman who didn't take it personally when business matters interrupted life. Nicole understood that my business was a part of me, integral to my life, not just something I did to make a living. She knew I was working because I was passionate about my company and needed to spend time on it, especially in the beginning stages, in order to transform it into a successful venture. She didn't begrudge me the long hours "at the office" or the "working weekends." When we went on our honeymoon more than five years after the launching of my business, it was not only the start of our married life, but it was also the first time in my twenties that I had taken more than two consecutive days of vacation.

During those first years of trials and many errors, I basically ate nothing but plain old jarred spaghetti sauce and pasta, eating out only when I took customers and potential customers out for meals. (Hopefully, they didn't notice the way I delved into a nonspaghetti entrée!) But working many hours and living frugally, especially during the first two years of business, enabled me to keep my small team confident of our future success, even though we were operating on a payroll-to-payroll basis.

Did I amble down all the right roads during my entrepreneurial journey? Hardly. I spent precious dollars (the last few hundred I had in the bank) on an airline ticket to Indianapolis to meet with a potential customer, only to be ungraciously stood up. I wrecked a rented Ryder truck that I was driving because we couldn't afford to pay professionals to pick up some new manufacturing equipment that we needed—

thank God for insurance. An electrical fire erupted because I could not afford to hire a bona fide electrician when we expanded our clean room. In the process of wiring the 480V panel myself, using an *Electrical Work for Dummies* book, I grounded two wires. To this day I still get shaky in the knees when I see someone doing electrical work. These are just three examples of the many hurdles that definitely were not in my game plan.

Don't Plan on It

In fact, if you look at my original business plan from 2001, the only aspect you might recognize is the name of the company. The path that my team and I took after the business began made many unforeseen turns. Like most novice entrepreneurs, I did not anticipate a competitive response to our business. But I learned this fact quickly: there is *always* a competitive response to a successful model.

How did competitors react to our small but emerging company when we started to generate a buzz in the biotech industry? Representatives of our largest competitor—one of the biggest companies in the world—periodically spread rumors that we were going out of business. Nothing like bankruptcy whispers to frighten away your customers! The tactic of our rivals that was my personal favorite was when they informed some of our customers that a "Big Company" was suing us, thus making future purchases from us risky.

Yet even through all this subterfuge and struggle, we survived and ultimately flourished. These hardships and obstacles, along with our ability to obstinately overcome them, meshed into our company's culture, our attitude, and our manner of reacting and progressing. We knew that the products we provided to the world were beneficial, and that fact helped us to rally when roadblocks surfaced.

By the time I sold Mitos, we were 40-people strong with almost $8 million in annualized revenue. We were not just a business, we were a team, a family that had labored hard and served well together.

There were many long and winding, divergent roads between the birth of a business idea and my handshake with

Mr. Kleepak six and a half years later. And, you know, even if I could, I would not skip a single one of those roads. Doing what I loved— founding a business I believed in and directing the whole operation—taught me more about myself than a roomful of psychology experts. Forging my own path helped me "find myself" as a man, as a person. Every challenge and setback forced me to grow up and learn quickly. I would not be the husband, father, son, brother, friend, mentor, or business associate I am today if I had not taken a risk and pursued my dream. I could have chosen a more traditional route after college, but I *knew*—without really comprehending why—that that route just was not for me.

Thankfully, I listened and responded to the call of my inner entrepreneur.

What you should know:

- *Whether you are starting a business from scratch, joining an early stage business, or building a new enterprise within an existing business, one outcome is guaranteed: your blueprint for the venture will not go exactly as you planned, no matter how much or how painstakingly you prepare. Remember that fact when challenges pop up.*
- *Entrepreneurial businesses will probably require more of your time and energy than you can possibly anticipate. So rest up and go get 'em!*
- *When the going gets tough, keep going.*
- *Succeed or fail, the art of trying to achieve your goal will prove beneficial to you. It will help you grow not only as a businessperson but also as a human being, especially if your business creates a product or service that adds value to society.*

Two

What Makes an Entrepreneur?

Nature versus Nurture

If someone succeeds, is it due to nature or nurture? That's a question that has been debated at great length. For idealists who believe that we control our own destiny, there is now overwhelming evidence suggesting that excelling does not come solely from innate gifts and, more importantly, the innate gifts to excel reside in all of us.

K. Anders Ericsson, professor of psychology at Florida State University, has dedicated much of his life to understanding why certain individuals excel while others do not. In study after study, Ericsson and his colleagues prove that success has more to do with what has been coined as "deliberate practice" than anything else. Of course, there are limitations to this theory. For example, someone who only grows to be five feet tall will probably never play in the NBA. However, Ericsson's research suggests that there are few such limitations to success.

Deliberating about Deliberate Practice

Most people reach a point in the development of a skill where the ability to increase their performance levels off. In my youth, I once told my parents about the law of diminishing returns as an explanation for why I earned B's on my report card. I reasoned that I had worked hard to achieve the B's and that while I probably could have earned A's, it would have required a tremendous amount of additional work. Using this logic, I had stumbled onto a key element regarding the difference between average performers and those who excel: excellence comes to those who are willing to continue to take extra steps to ensure they improve.

As Anders Ericsson noted: "Deliberate practice is about changing your performance, setting new goals and straining yourself to reach a bit higher each time. It involves you deciding to improve something and setting up training conditions to attain the skill."[1]

Practice and deliberate practice are worlds apart. To use a golf analogy, practice is going to the driving range and hitting 300 balls; deliberate practice is going to the driving range and focusing on hitting 300 pitching wedges 120 yards, with the goal of getting 75 percent within 50 feet of the hole. In other words, people who deliberately practice set goals provide themselves with feedback on their goals, make adjustment to their performance, and after reaching their goals, they once again elevate their goals. One of the reasons that golf is such a popular sport in our society is because it creates a unique opportunity in which one can compete against oneself in a very measurable way.

Deliberate practice itself is an acquired skill that requires constant development. It is developed by setting goals, executing with 100 percent commitment to achieving those goals, systematically reflecting upon the success or failure in achieving the goals, and then adjusting. This is the cornerstone of people's ability to achieve success in whatever field they choose.

The Non-Zero-Sum Game

In a non-zero-sum game, cooperation between two or more people leads to some greater gain for the group.[2] Basically, in a

---

1. Anna Patty, "Why only the right kind of practice gets anywhere near perfect," The Sydney Mornging Herald, May 15, 2006.

2 Beinhocker Eric. 2006 *The Origin of Wealth*. Boston, MA: Harvard Business School Press, p. 222/

zero-sum game, an economic pie is worth $10.When two parties interact, that pie's value remains at $10, which means if party A gets $7, party B only receives $3. Many people assume that the world operates on a zero-sum game. In reality, people make decisions each day that expand the $10 pie. For example, the right partnerships can create a valuable product or service for society and increase the value of a $10 pie to $15, leaving Party A with an $8 slice and Party B with a $7 slice, a success for both.

We often find ourselves in an environment where we talk about winning. However, winning is by definition a zero-sum game. There is a winner and a loser. But excelling or succeeding is often a non-zero-sum game.

I find it strange when people say how competitive they are, yet they put forth little of the effort or are unwilling to make the sacrifices needed to ensure success. Yes, they give it their best shot, and when they lose a competition, they scream and shout, which they consider competitive behavior. The issue is that these individuals are competing against an arbitrary scale. Think of it this way: a thirty-year-old who plays basketball against an eight-year-old and triumphs every time considers himself a winner. This mindset is flawed because the win is relative, based on the competitor, and it takes an extremely shortsighted view of winning. This flawed thinking is why we so often confuse winning with excelling or succeeding.

People who constantly compete against lesser opponents are unlikely to improve. As demonstrated throughout this book, learning comes as much from failures as it does from successes, and anyone who engages in only one side of this equation is likely to miss some very important lessons. Performing at one's peak level requires discipline and a commitment not only to play the game as hard as possible, but also to prepare before the game as thoroughly as possible. A single game or a single deal rarely makes a career. Instead, people who constantly elevate their games to compete at a higher and higher level make an impact on the world. For these individuals, competition comes from within.

Geoffrey Colvin summarizes it best in his 2006 Fortune article *What it takes to be great*; "The authors of a study on excelling in society conclude: 'We still do not know which factors encourage individuals to engage in deliberate practice.' Or as the University of Michigan Business School professor

Noel Tichy puts it after thirty years of working with managers: 'Some people are much more motivated than others, and that's the existential question I cannot answer—why.'"

The Roots of Passion and Purpose

So why was I willing to settle for B's as a child but, when I became an adult, went the extra mile to succeed as an entrepreneur? I believe the answer to this question and to Mr. Tichy's conundrum lies in a single word: *passion.* Almost every person I know who finds his or her passion also has an innate commitment to succeed and excel. This is why even successful entrepreneurs come back for more. Financially, they may have no reason to return to a job that requires tremendous hours and involves a high level of stress, yet they are passionate about entrepreneurship and want to continue to improve their performance. This passion comes from a deep-rooted, unconscious fulfillment of a need to have a purpose. While some academics may argue that passion does not always correlate with purpose, there is nevertheless a very strong connection between the two.

At almost every party or other social event I attend, at least one person approaches me to discuss a terrific idea he or she has for a business. More than anything else (except maybe family, religion, or politics), people are passionate about entrepreneurship. Why?

Like many questions, the answer lies in our past. Entrepreneurship is defined as an attempt to organize people and resources in new and more valuable ways. The term is typically associated with those who found a business; however, as evidenced by the definition, entrepreneurs exist in all parts of our society. The reason that so many people are excited about entrepreneurship is that while it offers an opportunity to make a living, it also provides purpose to help others, benefitting society as a whole and bringing value to the world that will live on for many years. In essence, entrepreneurship in all its many forms has increased the standard of living for people around the globe.

When I reflect on my early journey as an entrepreneur, I am amazed at how many people helped me in so many ways, without any financial reward. When I meet fellow entrepreneurs, they echo my experience. I believe that entrepreneurs who help other entrepreneurs along the entrepreneurial path subconsciously find purpose in assisting others, just like people in Teach for America find meaning in helping inner-city children, or ministers find joy in guiding people to a better life.

Throughout history, those who found purpose in life were more likely to be successful, to find a mate, and to support a family. Those who had no purpose in life, drifting aimlessly and focusing inward with no thought about the future, did little to elevate society and were therefore less likely to succeed.

Imagine two equal-sized tribes of early Europeans roaming the continent 7,000 years ago. Due to the randomness of evolution, a person born into tribe A finds purpose as a motivator. This purpose provides him with the passion to focus on improving his life and the lives of those around him. Throughout his thirty years, he develops means of organizing his tribe, which enables each member of the tribe to have specialized jobs. The ability to focus, practice, and perfect one's skills in a particular area provides constant incremental improvements in all areas. Most importantly, farming specialists devote themselves to intensive food production, thereby yielding surpluses to feed the nonproducers.[3]

This in turn allows more people to focus on aspects of life that are not related to food farming. Some work on perfecting the skill of hunting, which leads to better techniques and innovative new tools for hunting. Some work on construction and develop new and better ways to build shelter and structures to provide common defense, and so on.

Tribe B has no such motivator emerge from their group, and thus each person within the community continues individually to provide food, clothing, and shelter to his family, and the only real value of the tribe's togetherness is the unity of defense against other tribes. Over the years, tribe B members have developed less reliance upon each other and therefore are more likely to leave the tribe.

At the same time, because they develop specialists for farming, hunting, and construction, tribe A gains a higher

---

[3] Jared Diamond, *Guns, Germs and Steel* (New York: W.W. Norton & Company, 1997), 62.

standard of living for their people and are able to have more children and live longer. In addition, a high percentage of people (those who begin to develop a connection to and dependence on their fellow tribespeople) stay with the tribe, and new members are more likely to join in. The individual motivator who efficiently organizes the tribe most likely gains an elevated status within the community and produces a high number of offsprings who inherit his same genetic need for purpose, thus accelerating the differences between tribes A and B. Over generations, tribe B will eventually die off, while tribe A will continue to thrive. This dynamic provides us with an inherited trait that predisposes us to entrepreneurship and helps to drive us toward a life of purpose.

An American Tradition

Why does the United States excel at entrepreneurship over most other societies? This began centuries ago when America first represented a land of opportunity where a person could control his or her own destiny. Our lineage is filled with individuals who sought change, were unwilling to settle for the status quo, and found purpose in providing a better life for themselves and their family in a new country.

In the preindustrial era, the act of boarding a small boat that was packed with hundreds of people and setting off across the sea in hopes of arriving in America was a tremendously dangerous task that required great risk, tolerance, and sacrifice. These daring journeys required men, women, and children to live in small cots and hammocks packed together to maximize space during the long voyage. Food turned moldy and sour, and water became foul and undrinkable. The discomforts were nothing compared to the risks of survival. Childbirth, disease, and death in these tiny quarters were commonplace. Storms and pirates also claimed many ships during this journey that would typically take four to six weeks.

On arrival, it was understood that America was not the place to go if you wanted an easy life. America was a difficult environment for those unwilling to do menial jobs, and there was no welcome for the lazy. The immigrant was not asked what he was, but what he could do.[4]

---

[4] Terry Colman, *Passage to America* (England: Victorian Book Club, 1973).

These discomforts and risks were all well known, yet between 1820 and 1920, 33 million[5] immigrants arrived on the shores of America. They viewed this journey as a calculated risk in search of a better life for themselves and their families. Likewise, those who were happy with their lives or simply unwilling to take a great risk remained in their respective countries. Thus, compared to other nations in the world, America emerged as a country filled with a disproportionate number of calculated risk-takers. This culture has been self-reinforced because those who are not comfortable with calculated risk taking typically fail to flourish in the American culture. What has emerged is a society that admires hard work and calculated risk taking by those with a passion and purpose to excel. This is a key ingredient not only for successful start-up companies, but for our society as a whole.

From Purpose to Success

We are all born with a need for purpose. There are thousands of ways to fill this purpose, and entrepreneurship is one of them. For the remainder of this book we will use the term *entrepreneur* as a person who starts a business, but don't discount other entrepreneurs in your life. They may not start businesses, but they find effective ways to impact the world, such as teaching our youth, raising families, or performing lifesaving surgeries. Entrepreneurs include artists who show us beauty, and journalists whose unbiased stories provide us with guidance to learn about the world. Most importantly, don't forget those who go to work every day and make the small changes in the world that improve the standard of living for everyone. They include assembly-line workers who search for more efficient ways to build a motor or computer hackers who develop a new code to make online research faster and easier. Entrepreneurs, no matter which hat we wear, are all members of society, moving forward together, and each giving to the world around us in our own unique way.

No matter how your entrepreneurial streak plays out, to be truly successful at anything, you need to have passion for it.

---

[5] Kim, Sukko, 1997 Immigration, Industrial Revolution and Urban Growth in the United States 1820–1920, Washington University in St. Louis

Without passion, you will not consider the hurdles you encounter as the stepping stones of deliberate practice. Entrepreneurship requires a constant attempt to improve performance, to compete against oneself to achieve to the best of one's ability.

We are all born with a need for purpose. This need for purpose supports or often develops our passion. And passion provides the motivation to elevate our performance and continues to turn our inherited traits into the skills required for success. Skills make us successful at what we do.

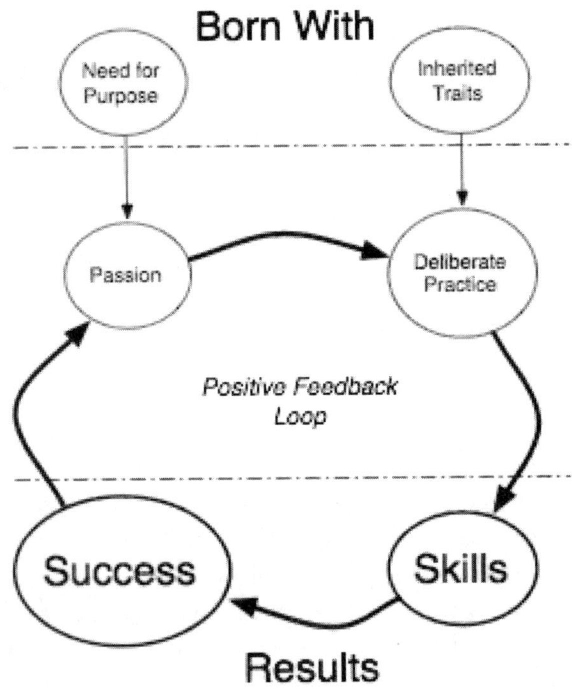

If entrepreneurship provides this purpose, you will find your passion and be ready to continue your journey as an entrepreneur.

What you should know:

- *Recognize that your entrepreneurial zeal is in your heritage and in your DNA.*

- *Develop the skill of deliberate practice to compete against yourself and continually improve.*
- *Find and pursue your passion.*

Three

Sharpening Your Entrepreneurial Skills

You will read the stories of successful entrepreneurs highlighted throughout this book. Their paths and ideas differ greatly, but their common thread is that they took their inherited traits and dedicated themselves to turning those traits into the skills needed to succeed. Once they developed these skills, they continued to improve upon them daily. This improvement process was often undefined, but they laid out their goals, measured themselves against these goals, and reviewed the reasons for their successes and failures. Regardless of the outcome of their entrepreneurial venture, they focused on future improvement.

For the sake of clarity, we will refer to a trait as something that someone is born with, and a skill as something that is developed over time through knowledge and experience.

The Building Blocks

Mel Baiada and Mark Loschiavo of the Baiada Entrepreneurship Center at Drexel University have worked tirelessly to identify the key traits of successful entrepreneurs, and they have ascertained how to enhance these traits in our youth.

The idea for *We Are All Born Entrepreneurs* was the result of a Mark Loschiavo lecture featuring the traits of successful entrepreneurs. After the lecture, while playing with my eighteen-month-old daughter, I noticed that all of the characteristics Mark mentioned were apparent in my little girl—and in almost all young children. While the argument of nature versus nurture continues, anyone who has spent time with children notices that youngsters possess most of the entrepreneurial traits outlined by Mark. Every child has a varying level of competence in each of these areas, and, over time, environmental factors begin to influence them dramatically; however, as a base, the entrepreneurial traits are present in most children, which means they are innate to everyone.

Entrepreneurial Traits

The traits that Mel and Mark identified include the following:

- **Locus of control**: A psychological term, locus of control refers to a person's belief about what causes the good or bad results in his or her life, either in general or in a specific area, such as health or academics. It can either be internal (meaning individuals believe that they control themselves and their life) or external (meaning individuals believe that their environment, some higher power, or other people control their decisions and their life). In general, people who have an internal locus of control are more apt to become successful entrepreneurs, mainly because they have the ability to depict cause-and-effect outcomes in their decisions.

When my wife was twelve, she fervently wanted to take horseback-riding lessons. Her parents said that she could have the lessons, but only if she paid for them. She quickly discovered that horseback-riding lessons were very expensive and told her parents that she did not have enough money to cover them. That's a shame, they said, which made my wife realize that it was solely up to her to find some way to pay for the riding lessons. Determined, she approached the stable's owner and asked for a discount on the lessons. Eventually, she and the owner negotiated a deal, whereby she cleaned the horse stalls once a week in return for a riding lesson. While I am sure that my in-laws could have afforded the lessons, they chose to let their daughter determine her own course. That twelve-year-old girl learned several important lessons, including the fact that her fate was up to her, and there are always outside-the-box options.

- **Singularity of purpose:** This is defined as the cognitive awareness in linking cause and effect for achieving a goal. In general, the anticipated result guides decision making in choosing appropriate actions within a range of strategies based on varying degrees of ambiguity. Purpose serves to change the state of conditions in a given environment, usually to one with a perceived improvement from the previous state. This change is the motivation that serves the locus of control and goal orientation.

Children not only understand cause and effect at a young age, but they are also enthralled by it. Just look at the smile on the faces of children the first time they flip on a light switch and realize that they control the ability to create light. While all children possess curiosity about this cause-and-effect relationship, successful entrepreneurs develop this skill set throughout their lives and expand it to include not only the cause and effect of a single action, but of complex systems with immeasurable variables. I don't think it is a coincidence that many entrepreneurs grow up playing strategy games like Risk and Stratego. At an early age, these games enhanced their ability to map out complex situations and choose a course of action that provided the best chance of success.

- **Ambiguity tolerance:** *"This includes the ability to perceive ambiguity in information and behavior in a neutral and open* *way. In psychology and management, tolerance of ambiguity levels are correlated with creativity, risk aversion, psychological resilience, lifestyle, orientation toward diversity (cross-cultural communication and intercultural competence), and leadership style. David Wilkinson's Modes of Leadership, as explained in The Ambiguity Advantage (2006), is largely based on ambiguity tolerance. Mode one leaders have the least tolerance to ambiguity, with mode four leaders enjoying and preferring to work in ambiguous situations. In part, mode four types thrive in uncertain circumstances due to what Wilkinson calls "emotional resilience." The converse, ambiguity intolerance, which was introduced in The Authoritarian Personality in 1950, is defined as a 'tendency to perceive or interpret information marked by vague, incomplete, fragmented, multiple, probable, unstructured, uncertain, inconsistent, contrary, contradictory, or unclear meanings as actual or potential sources of psychological discomfort or threat.'"*[6] Entrepreneurs must constantly move forward with incomplete information; if they are unwilling to do so, they remain frozen. In a later chapter, you will learn that one of the keys to entrepreneurial success is finding a means of removing ambiguity as quickly and cost-effectively as possible.

Children start out in the world as a blank slate, so everything represents ambiguity to them. Yet most children are comfortable experiencing the unknown in their world. Eventually, they are taught to have all of the necessary information on hand before acting. In our complex and quickly evolving world, however, total information simply does not exist. Because circumstances are constantly fluid, if entrepreneurs hesitate to act until they have 100 percent of the required information, they will fail to progress.

- **Need to achieve and learn:** For more than twenty years, Harvard University's David C. McClelland has

---

6. Wikipedia, "Ambiguity tolerance," http://en.wikipedia.org/wiki/Ambiguity_tolerance (accessed Feb, 2nd 2009)

studied the urge to achieve. His research led him to believe that the need to achieve is a distinct human motive that other creatures in the universe do not possess. Every successful entrepreneur I have met possesses this need to achieve, to be the best that they can be. Without this drive, people accept failure; with it, entrepreneurs view failure as part of their practice and the learning process, and they forge ahead.

There are few greater experiences in a person's life than watching his or her child learn. Whether they are learning to walk, speak, read, or build a tower of blocks, children have an unmatched, natural joy in achieving and learning. And if they stumble when they first start to walk or stutter when they begin to talk, they soldier on and continue trying with each step and every word. Young children crave knowledge and absorb each new detail in their lives—learning how to tie a shoe, watching a bird in the backyard, discovering an uncovered treasure in an Easter egg hunt—with unadulterated glee.

➢ **Resilience:** This describes the positive capacity of people to cope with stress and catastrophe. As evidenced by the entrepreneurial stories throughout this book, life never unfolds as planned, and it is critical to bounce back from adversity. Entrepreneurs tend to be like a child's "Punching Bob." When this toy is punched, it is knocked to the floor, but immediately bounces upright.

My eighteen-month-old daughter knows no fear. I once watched her place a rigid, four-legged child's chair on top of a soft couch in hopes of gaining a better view of what was going on outside in our yard. She relentlessly climbed on top of the couch and repeatedly attempted to sit on the chair, only to see the chair fall to the ground each time that she tried to settle into it. Finally, after many attempts, she was able to place the chair on top of the couch and sit in it. But her pride of accomplishment was short-lived as she and the chair soon crashed to the ground. After some tears, she was right back at it, resiliently trying once again to place the chair on the couch to look at the world outside.

Most successful entrepreneurs with whom I have spoken remember facing a failure or two in their youth, picking themselves up off the ground, and starting over. Their parents didn't rescue them; instead, the parents allowed them to fail and to learn from the experience. The ability to bounce back from a failure reinforced the young entrepreneurs' confidence and natural resilience. Conversely, I suspect that children whose parents protect them to the point of fixing all of their failures lose the natural tendency to meet life's challenges. These are the parents who stay up all night to create their child's science fair project or give their teenager a credit card with no limits. The kids never encounter a problem or face failure because their parents shield them from all adversity. These children grow up to become adults who are unfamiliar with any type of failure, rejection, or criticism.

- **Connectedness:** This is associated with or relating to others. *"According to Dr. Edward M. Hallowell in an essay of the same name, connectedness is a sense of being a part of something larger than oneself, a feeling of belonging or accompaniment."*[7] It is that feeling in your bones that you are not alone. It is a sense that, even during a crisis, there is someone for you to lean on and to help you navigate through troubled waters. While ambition drives us to achieve, connectedness is the force that urges us to ally, affiliate, enter into mutual relationships, take strength, and grow through cooperative behavior.

Children enter the world with a strong connectedness to their parents. This is why even a simple hug from mom or dad can often solve all problems. As children progress in the right environment, the circle of connectedness grows to include extended family, friends, and, for the truly fortunate, a link to all members of society.

Groundwork for the Future

Mel and Mark's work is critical to strengthening entrepreneurial traits in our children. Not only do entrepreneurs bring tremendous value to society, they tend to be some of its

---

[7] First Serve Strategies, "Youth Experiences: Influences on entrepreneurial success," Evanston Public Library, www.firstserves.com/Youth%20Experiences.doc

happiest and most fulfilled people, mainly because they satisfy their sense of purpose. For these reasons, we owe it to future generations to understand entrepreneurial traits and help develop them into skills. As you will see throughout this book, these basic traits—which were transformed into skills—allowed me and other entrepreneurs to become successful.

It is up to us to develop these traits in ourselves as well as unleash them in others. We must instill in the next generation an understanding that they can control their own destiny and follow their passions, viewing missteps or failures as necessary learning steps.

Societal evolution has ensured that children possess entrepreneurial traits, unencumbered by the restrictions or prejudices of the world. If these characteristics exist in almost everyone as a child, then they inherently exist in all of us. But although we are born with these traits, constant, deliberate practice is required to transform them into strong entrepreneurial skills.

Over a dozen entrepreneurs are highlighted in this book, and while each person's story and path are unique, at base level, they all share two encompassing skills that can be tied directly to their base inherited traits: (1) calculated risk-taking; and (2) confident leadership.

Entrepreneurial Skills

- **Calculated Risk Taking:** This encompasses the ability to map different outcomes in a world with an immeasurable amount of variables and effectively prioritize while also understanding and estimating the risk and reward for each outcome; it then involves selecting the path that leads to the desired outcome, all the while juggling short-term needs with long-term goals. Calculated risk taking is derived from our locus of control, singularity of purpose, and ambiguity tolerance.

You may have heard the saying "ideas are free," and for the most part this is true. However, turning an idea into a product or service and then into a business is far from easy—or free. Most people have aspirations or dreams, but successful entrepreneurs transform dreams into reality. Entrepreneurs have the ability to identify a need in the marketplace and organize the complex steps required to fill that need with an appropriate product or service. Along the way, entrepreneurs also have the flexibility to adjust their original plan as information and market conditions change, and to achieve results from calculated risk taking, all the while using a finite amount of resources.

I once met a young entrepreneur—I'll call him John Doe—who had a tremendous idea that could have provided value for potential customers. John also had the unique ability to vividly describe how his product would impact the world, painting a picture that entailed millions of people using his invention every day. John's idea was a winner, but his dream never turned into reality because he was unable to map out the small steps to develop his concept—with no tangible product, no infrastructure or customers—to a final product that customers could use. As a result, John's dream never came to fruition.

The Amazing Amazon

In the mid-1990s, it eventually became apparent that Internet retail was growing into a huge business, but not everyone profited from the trend. Most Internet retail businesses went completely bust. But although there were venture capitalists who lost billions of dollars in Internet retail companies, some of today's most respected retailers also emerged from the fray. Most notable among this group was Amazon, which evolved into one of the country's top online retailers. Amazon's journey was not without its bumps, but its founder, Jeff Bezos, navigated through a quickly changing market more deftly than his competitors. He was able to paint a picture of a future state and build the thousands of intermediate steps needed to reach his goal. Early on, he focused solely on growth; the company had T-shirts made with the motto, "Eat another hot dog, get big fast!" And they certainly did "get big fast," growing more quickly than any other online marketer. But, like so many other success stories, when circumstances in the market changed, Amazon did not continue to blindly follow the same path; instead, they adjusted course. In 2001, after losing $1.4 billion and acknowledging that financial markets would no longer fund enormous losses, Bezos changed his strategy. The company cut its staff, focused on its core businesses, and developed strategic partnerships to provide more capital-efficient growth. Today, Amazon provides the world with an efficient means of purchasing items online and successfully services approximately forty million customers.

This extremely condensed version of Amazon's emergence demonstrates Jeff Bezos' ability to take calculated risks. Bezos navigated Internet marketing by building a plan and making calculated divergences from his original idea in order to reach the desired outcome (singularity of purpose). Throughout the company's ups and downs, he kept control of his own fate by making personal and professional sacrifices and balancing long-term goals with short-term needs (locus of control). Bezos also measured risks and made appropriate decisions with limited information (ambiguity tolerance).

- **Confident Leadership:** This is the ability to have others follow a constantly unstable and diverging path without all the answers, to engage individuals in a process or concept that is larger than any one person. The skill is derived from a desire to achieve, and from practicing resilience, ambiguity tolerance, and connectedness.

There is hardly a business idea in existence that you can't shoot a thousand holes into, yet entrepreneurs persevere and succeed every day. Perhaps the most difficult challenge that entrepreneurs face is the ability to listen to input from others while developing the confidence to move forward in what is generally considered a very risky proposition. Whether it is customers, employees, suppliers, or financiers, entrepreneurs need to lead others down unknown paths. This cannot be accomplished without confident leadership.

Listen to Audible's Story

As I sat with founder Don Katz at the corporate headquarters of Audible in Newark, New Jersey, I was unprepared to hear the roller-coaster history of his company. Audible currently employs 185 people, produces $60 million-plus in revenue, and has emerged as the market leader in digital book sales. Audible's product is a clear winner in the technology market, and it allows books and other verbal or written materials, such as magazines and speeches, to be downloaded at a fraction of the price of producing cassettes or CDs. Fourteen years after starting Audible, Don can proudly reflect on his company's growth and know that it changed the market.

But the journey Don took in life was certainly not one he would have predicted. The son of a successful entrepreneur, Don was an accomplished freelance writer and author of several best-selling books. In addition to concentrating on his writing career, Don also found an effective way to promote his work by learning as much as he could about the ins and outs of the publishing industry.

While working closely with his daughter to help her deal with dyslexia, Don noticed the powerful synchronization between audio and visual learning. His daughter's ability to listen to books as she was reading them was one of the key components that encouraged her to persevere. As a result, Don began to investigate a small segment of the publishing world that produced books on tape. What he found was a highly inefficient market that he believed could benefit from the technology revolution hovering on the horizon. Thus the Audible company was born. When I asked Don what prepared him for starting a new company, he smiled and said: "No one is more entrepreneurial than a freelance writer with a mortgage."

Don proceeded to contact his old college roommate, a computer science major. With Don's understanding of the publishing industry and his former roommate's technological expertise, they developed the concept for an audible book that could be downloaded to an audio book player. With a team of six people working in a former medical office, Audible raised funds, first with an angel investor and then with venture capitalists.

Like many great entrepreneurs, Don was slightly ahead of his time. When Audible's product development was completed in 1997, the market was simply not ready for digital media. Consumers were still using dial-up connections, which made downloading books a very slow process. People were not yet comfortable using credit cards on the Internet, and the original Audible device was simply too expensive for the buying public.

So how did they survive? Fortunately, everything digital was booming at the time, and investors could not get enough of digital products. In 1999, with only 3,000 customers, Audible went public.

Fasten Your Seat Belts, It's Going to be a Bumpy Ride

Between 2001 and 2003, Audible almost went bankrupt and several times had to lay off a significant portion of their work force. In addition to the financial whirlwind, on two separate occasions, Don felt that the organization needed a leader with different skills, and he brought in individuals to replace him as CEO.

At one point, a third of the company was sold to Microsoft. As the company's value shrank below the NASDAQ minimum of $10 million (down from a $650 million IPO value), Audible was delisted from the stock exchange. APEX, a private equity firm, eventually stepped in and purchased Microsoft's share of the company. This scenario continued until 2003 when Don received a call from Apple Computer's Steve Jobs, who said he was interested in developing a device to carry audible content. Miraculously, the birth of the iPod provided new life for the struggling Audible.

Today, it is easy to describe Audible's success and its obvious value proposition. As Don states, "We give our customers hundreds of hours a year in extra reading. The value of time is a key to a lot of great products." Audible began with bootstrapping, raised funds from angel investors, was backed by several venture capitalists, IPO'ed on the NASDAQ, was delisted from the NASDAQ, sold a major stake to Microsoft, sold a large portion of the company to a private equity firm, and then was sold in its entirely to one of the largest, most successful organizations in the world, Amazon. Don has lived the entrepreneurial equivalent of nine lives over the past fourteen years.

Follow the Leader

So what is confident leadership? Don Katz exemplifies it. Don saw a clear need in the marketplace and stopped at nothing to achieve it (desire to achieve). He was knocked down several times, but continued to rise again. In his entrepreneurial venture, the path changed several times due to many factors outside of his control. Through this mountain of challenges, Don kept customers, employees, investors, and suppliers moving down a path together (resilience).

He was comfortable making decisions and moving forward, even though he did not have all the answers (ambiguity tolerance). Like most successful leaders, Don inherently understood that we are all part of the world, bound together with fellow humans to fulfill a purpose. Embedding this understanding into his power of persuasion, he was able to motivate and connect with others to achieve results (connectedness).

It's All up to You

To develop these skills, entrepreneurs must engage in constant, deliberate practice in which they establish goals, attempt to meet those goals, reflect on past successes and failures, develop an understanding of what they did correctly and incorrectly, and create means of ensuring that their past experiences will help them meet future challenges. This process forces the development of calculated risk taking and confident leadership. (The process will be more thoroughly addressed in chapter 8.)

If you are truly passionate about excelling in entrepreneurship, it is critical that you continually enhance the skills mentioned above. To evolve as a successful entrepreneur requires exercising your mind, placing yourself in situations where you have an opportunity to test your skills, leaving your comfort zone, and even failing occasionally

What you should know:

- *We all possess the traits required to succeed as entrepreneurs.*
- *To be successful, develop the skills of calculated risk taking and confident leadership.*
- *Developing the necessary skills requires constant practice and effective self-reflection.*

Four

The Early Road to Entrepreneurship

Rudy Wolfs knew he didn't want to work as a housepainter, so by age fourteen, he decided to become an entrepreneur.

It all began with Rudy's family's busy contracting business. The oldest son of three boys, he was thirteen when the family business landed a lucrative contract to paint eight schools over the summer break. Rudy was assigned to perform all of the taping around the edges of the walls so the painters could come in and quickly get to work. So every weekday morning, he rose early, rode his bike to the job site, strapped on his knee pads, and started taping. Over the course of three months, Rudy completely wore through three sets of knee pads and decided that the life of a painter was not for him!

Watching his parents grow their contracting business, however, taught him three very important lessons: (1) More work yields more rewards; (2) Only you control your success; and (3) It's crucial to keep learning new skills.

Of course, the family's business had its ups and downs, but Rudy realized that there was a direct correlation between the amount of time that his parents worked on the business and the financial rewards that followed.

He also observed that his father was in a feast-or-famine environment in which he constantly had to learn new skills in order to respond to customer demand and survive. For instance, equipment and techniques changed quite often due to technology and customer needs. One of the keys to Rudy's father's success was his ability to develop the right skills at the right time based on customer trends.

So at a very young age, Rudy embraced this notion of constantly acquiring new skills. When he was thirteen and his father told him that some customers would not accept handwritten invoices, Rudy quickly volunteered to figure out how to solve the problem.

At the time, he basically knew nothing about computers. It was the mid-1980s and Apple 2 had just hit the market. So Rudy purchased one, along with some basic programming books, and began to develop a way to create electronic invoices. After learning the basics of programming and accounting (yes, at the age of thirteen), he eventually produced a program that generated invoices and accounts receivable reports for his father.

Rudy loved the challenge of creating a product that filled a need for his family's business. By the age of fourteen, he also realized that many of his father's friends with plumbing, electrical, and carpentry businesses had the same need for an electronic accounting system. So Rudy formed a business that was later called EveryWare Development and went on to build accounting software solutions for his dad's buddies.

By the time he was nineteen, Rudy had turned down a college swimming scholarship and decided to dedicate himself to building his business instead of pursuing a degree. At the time, his software company had eight employees, and Rudy realized that he needed to add other partners with complementary skills. First he brought on equity partners with experience in technology, sales, and marketing. Then, when he was in his early twenties, the ever self-aware Rudy stepped down as CEO and became CTO when the company raised money on the public equity markets. By the late 1990s, when EveryWare was sold, it had 120 employees and $10 million in revenue.

Rudy's path is truly unique for two reasons. I don't know of any other company that was founded by a fourteen-year-old and ended up going public, and few entrepreneurs transition from working for themselves to working for another company. But Rudy is the exception. For a number of years, the CEO of

ING DIRECT, an online bank, had been a loyal EveryWare customer. ING DIRECT's CEO (Arkadi Kuhlmann) was a dynamic leader whose vision to reinvent financial services was outrageous and contagious. After EveryWare was sold, Rudy accepted a one-year consulting contract to launch ING DIRECT in the United States, and for the first time in his adult life, this thirty-something had a boss. He approached the opportunity as an entrepreneur, invested in infrastructure like he was spending his own money and attacked every problem with a fresh perspective without the burden of a corporate background. The thrill of learning new skills and achieving unimaginable milestones was as rewarding as the money he was paid. Arkadi's drive and experience provided Rudy with a mentor that paved the way for great success.

Ten years later, Rudy is proud of what ING DIRECT has built from scratch and how much he has learned over the past decade. Today Rudy is the CIO of ING DIRECT with over $80 billion in assets, 7.5 million customers, and 2,300 employees. Rudy approaches each year as if his company were a start-up, continues to learn, and lives the entrepreneurs' dream within a corporate institution.

Like all successful entrepreneurs, Rudy is a true lifetime learner, one who considers his past experiences as stepping stones in his own development and who constantly practices for his next great business adventure.

My first entrepreneurial experience was much less successful than Rudy's, but it was no less significant in my development. At the time, my parents and brothers were tennis enthusiasts, and when I examined the stringer they frequently used to mend their tennis racquets, I thought to myself: "I can do that!" And so, at eleven years old, I did, creating flyers that heralded my services as a racquet stringer and posting them at local tennis courts. By the end of my first year of business, I had met dozens of new people, strung over 200 racquets at a profit of $10 per racquet, and caught a rock solid case of entrepreneurial fever.

Feedback Loops

A feedback loop is one in which a result generates another result in the same direction, continuing to spiral in that direction. Positive and negative feedback loops exist in mathematics, economics, and psychological systems. It's natural for people to work in areas where they excel and find passion for projects in which they succeed. These successes are what create positive feedback loops.

Most successful entrepreneurs I know recall an early time in their life where they were successful at a small entrepreneurial project. This is not a coincidence and why it's critical for aspiring entrepreneurs, as part of their deliberate practices, to develop modest projects in which they can find entrepreneurial success.

I did it by working a variety of jobs. In the early 1990s, when I was sixteen and had just bought my first car, I landed a job at Wall to Wall Sound and Video in the mall. I was a store clerk, which meant that I basically helped people find CDs or albums. I worked a total of 12 hours a week after school, making minimum wage, which was $4.15 an hour. I enjoyed the job for about three weeks, and then I received my first paycheck. I had worked about 20 hours and, after taxes were deducted, my pay was about $50. I remember doing the math in my head and figuring that I could have strung five tennis racquets in two and a half hours to bring home the same amount of money. With that in mind, I quickly resigned, graciously informing the store that I would stay on until they found a replacement. After that, I focused my efforts on stringing tennis racquets because I wanted to control my own destiny and garner the best return on my time.

My parents were always supportive of my crazy ideas. They understood that my entrepreneurial ventures were part of my education. They encouraged me to try new ideas and allowed me to learn more than a few lessons on my own. When I slipped up, they didn't point fingers, but guided me to reach an understanding of my missteps. As is true with most people, I learned better when I made my own discoveries as opposed to being told what I was *supposed* to learn. Absorbing the process of self-reflection allowed me to develop a true understanding of myself, my strengths, and my limitations. Essentially, my parents enabled me to plot my own course; for example, they didn't chastise me when I resigned from Wall to Wall; they simply asked why I did. They congratulated me when I succeeded, but did not provide false praise if I did a mediocre job. At home, my father and I played strategy games endlessly. Although they were recreational, these games were also the practices that allowed me to transform my inherent traits into the skills I would need later as an entrepreneur. Basically, they quietly mentored me, and their subtle leadership seeped into me. I don't recall exactly what toy or video game my parents gave me on a certain Christmas or birthday when I was a kid, but I vividly remember how they nurtured my skills and believed in me when I was young, and for that I am forever grateful.

My mother also encouraged me to be involved in the community. As a teacher and the daughter of a teacher and a librarian, she spent her youth establishing strong roots and developing a deep understanding of community. As a young teenager, I spent hours in the classroom with her, helping her teach everyone from energetic first graders to older children with learning disabilities. From watching her, I learned the joy of community and the importance of doing what you love. Following her example, I was involved in community groups such as Adopt-A-Highway and student government. Working with these groups provided me with lessons about organization and cooperative behavior.

With guidance from those around me, I used my successes in various areas to create a positive feedback loop, which, in turn, fired up my passion and encouraged me to want to learn more.

Failure—The Learning Process

While taking classes during a lazy summer at Penn State, my good friend David Suarez devised an idea that we hoped would cover our expenses for the summer and possibly create a big opportunity in the fall. At Penn State, he noticed, every college freshman arrived at his or her dorm for the first time to find a very sterile and cold room. No parents felt comfortable leaving their children in the bare room with painted block walls and a tile floor. While we never performed any surveys or market studies, we estimated that well over half of the students bought a carpet to brighten up their surroundings by the end of the first week of school. David and I had very little money, but we met with the owners of several large carpet stores until we found one that sold us 25 carpets at a discount of $30 each (the most my credit card could purchase) and allowed us to return any unsold carpets by the end of the day. So we loaded up my Ford Ranger with carpets and set out to find some prime Penn State real estate. We parked in the middle of campus and started selling the carpets for $40. By the time we had sold all but ten of the carpets, we realized that our price was too low, so we raised it to $50. The remaining ten carpets all sold within a few hours, and David and I had a summer's worth of beer money. We also had an idea of how to expand our enterprise in the fall when the number of students arriving at campus would increase tenfold.

That fall, we cut a deal with the same carpet store owner, but this time we purchased 250 carpets. We used our volume to get him to lower the price to $20 each; however, there was no return policy this time because he was concerned about being stuck with too many carpets. This was a final-sale deal.

David and I hired three friends to help us, and we all rolled up to campus in five Ryder trucks with the intention of doubling our money on that beautiful fall day. As soon as the first truck reached campus, security personnel not-so-politely asked us to vacate the premises. While I consider myself a good negotiator, I was out of my league against the seventy-five-year-old campus security guard who had been at Penn State as long as the legendary football coach Joe Paterno, or Joe Pa. As our friends exited the campus, waiting for David and me to create Plan B, I wondered how I was going to tell my parents that I had to skip a semester due to financial losses. Fortunately, Plan B worked, and we ended the day without a catastrophe, with a very modest loss, and with free carpets for all of our friends (and any cute girls who happened to walk down the street). Most importantly, we escaped with many lessons learned, and I had the time of my life.

I would be kidding myself to think that I found purpose in our carpet-selling venture, but I certainly was passionate about it. My passion had little to do with the potential of making money and more to do with the excitement of the entire project, including swimming out into unchartered waters and learning from the experience. Selling the carpets was part of my deliberate practice and a step toward increasing the skills that later enabled me to succeed as an entrepreneur. While I certainly didn't realize it at the time, it helped me to find my true purpose in life. Others may have viewed our endeavor as a failure, but David and I were pleased that we attempted to bring value by providing college students with carpets conveniently and cost-efficiently.

History's Dilemma

It was not until relatively recently in history that society's structure evolved to the point where it conflicted with our natural entrepreneurial DNA. In the twenty-first century, industrialization and technology have progressed so that many people employed by companies and governments work in extremely specialized roles, have responsibilities with a narrow focus, and use only specific skills. This trend toward specialization has generated excellence and innovation at a rate the world has never before witnessed, which has propelled worldwide growth, created greater opportunity for entrepreneurs, and allowed individuals to bring tremendous value to the world.

The Conflict

So the good news is that we no longer roam the earth looking for caves to live in and animals to hunt for food. The not-so-great news is that we have transformed into a structured world where most of us are surrounded by limits. Today, as a child marches through life, these limits proliferate and often turn into obstacles. Please do not misunderstand—society needs rules, and without regulations, chaos would reign. Nevertheless, as a person matures, it becomes difficult to peer over these obstacles and remember what life was like during childhood when testing limits and exploring the world was acceptable. A child enters the world with no baggage, but after decades of being told what to do and where to go, the innate desire to plot one's own course is beaten out of most individuals. Or is it? Perhaps it is just beaten *down,* hidden deep in one's soul. I say this because, as already mentioned, almost all individuals I have ever talked to, once they realize my background, want to brainstorm about a brilliant idea they have for a new business. This is almost without exception, which leads me to believe that the two-year-old curious, enterprising child still resides in us all.

The Opportunity

Now, more than any time in the history of the world, opportunity awaits entrepreneurs. Technology and society have evolved to a point where it is becoming easier and easier to unlock this hidden entrepreneur in everyone. Governments now understand that entrepreneurial innovation creates good jobs and are developing means of assisting early stage businesses. Almost every major college across the country is creating or has created entrepreneurship courses, and there are organizations such as Junior Achievement that introduce the business community to students at a very young age. And perhaps most importantly, the cost of starting a business has shrunk significantly in the past decade.

Where Is Everybody?

With so many drivers pushing people who have a passion for starting a business, why aren't more people taking a chance or looking to join early stage ventures? The two most common answers to this question from those who consider themselves entrepreneurs are: (1) I don't want to take the risk; and (2) I'm not experienced enough.

(1) **I do not want to take the risk.** This is a legitimate concern, not so much due to a fear of failure as to the impact of those failures at certain points in a person's life. I think the greatest risk is not starting a business if you are passionate about it *and* your personal circumstances allow it. In addition, working for huge corporations is hardly considered "safe" anymore. Behemoth corporations like Lehman Brothers have gone bankrupt, and large companies shed 75,000 jobs on January 26, 2009, alone. But while I do not believe risk is the real issue for most entrepreneurs, I do think the timing has to be right. Starting a business involves blood, sweat, and tears. It will require hundred-hour work weeks and will provide almost zero or even

negative pay. Now that I am married with a child, the idea of working a hundred hours a week has almost zero appeal because it would take time away from my family. Starting a business requires 100 percent focus from the founders, and, for many reasons, life circumstances will not justify this intense focus. If you are unable to make a full commitment, wait until the timing is right; in the meantime, don't sit idle; continue to build your skills, and map out a plan for future opportunities when your circumstances are more conducive to new endeavors.

(2) **I do not have enough experience.** This can be a logical concern, but is probably less valid than most people think. Obviously, a two-year-old cannot start a business, so there is some experience threshold that entrepreneurs must pass. But in my experience, this threshold has more to do with a person's ability to self-reflect than his or her resume. I was twenty-one when I started the carpet-selling business at Penn State. At that time, I was a pure optimist, only able to envision success in any idea that I created. It took failing and succeeding at selling carpets and many other small ventures for me to think through the weaknesses or potential downsides to my "big ideas" and accurately assess possible risks. I also did not seek enough help from more experienced individuals. I began to recognize some trends in my own thoughts, such as my tendency to oversimplify matters and my failure to thoroughly plan out details. I also realized that I seldom anticipated a competitive response and, as a result, rarely developed contingency plans. By the time I started Mitos at the age of twenty-three, I was much more aware of all these issues. To counter them, I found strong mentors, and I bounced my ideas off anyone who would listen. Because of my growing self-awareness, I was able to build a much more realistic business plan, and, most importantly, I surrounded myself with others who compensated for my shortcomings.

Know Thyself

Self-awareness springs from self-reflection, which is one of the key ingredients to deliberate practice. Self-reflection provides people with the ability to reflect and accurately assess their own strengths and limitations by reviewing the goals they have set and how they measure up against these goals. Reflection is a critical element in the development of one's skills. We learn what we are capable of by pushing our own limits and from our successes and failures; we develop a better understanding of our own strengths and weaknesses.

I know many forty-year-olds who do not possess self-reflection; however, through my involvement with DreamIt Ventures, an early stage venture fund, I have been exposed to eighteen-year-olds awash in it. So, rather than focusing solely on experience, I think it is better to focus on your own situation. If you truly develop the ability to reflect, you will be ready to start a business. This doesn't mean that you won't make mistakes; it simply means that you will learn from them and adjust for the future.

It's true that most people become wiser with experience and are more likely to succeed if they accurately reflect and learn from their past. However, I think it depends on a person's particular experience. For example, many entry-level positions encompass a very narrow focus, but starting a business from scratch requires a very broad focus. In my first job after college, my responsibility was to sell a product, which required a very narrow focus. During my first year at Mitos, however, I was the salesperson, product-design engineer, supply-chain manager, accountant, office manager, HR manager, customer-service rep, marketing director, assembly-line worker, process engineer, lawyer, business-development manager, and janitor.

At that first job, I learned a great deal about the selling process and developed an understanding of the basic way in which a business operates. That's because young people are like sponges and quickly absorb everything around them. I only spent about a year at my first job after college, but it was one of the most educational periods of my life, and I would not be where I am today without it.

Prime Time

Flipping the idea of experience on its head, it makes sense to start a business when you are young because you have nothing to lose. Although this book focuses on the positive aspects of becoming an entrepreneur, it is important to note that a high percentage of new businesses fail. That is a tough pill to swallow, but it is undoubtedly easier to fail when you are young and can bounce back from the experience without causing much harm to you or your loved ones.

Whether they succeed or fail, entrepreneurs learn the most on their first ventures. The earlier this happens, the more they will be able to draw on these experiences throughout their lifetime. If an entrepreneur is successful, the financial rewards deliver a standard of living that can be enjoyed for many years to come.

If you are passionate about entrepreneurship, there are many advantages to life as an entrepreneur and few reasons not to give it a shot.

What you should know:

- *Look for opportunities to enhance your skills. There are many ways an individual can become engaged in small organizations where they can learn, including nonprofits and community organizations.*
- *The best entrepreneurs that I know have failed in life. It is these failures that taught them what they needed to know about themselves. Knowing yourself is one of the most important aspects of growth.*
- *Search around for learning experiences; take small chances to learn the process of starting a business or turning an idea into a product.*
- *There are certain times in life when taking a risk is advantageous. Find and plan for these occasions.*

Five

The Real World

Although my stint in the corporate world seems like a panel straight out of a Dilbert cartoon, for a brief time, it was my life.

I was about twenty years old and had just completed the first semester of my sophomore year at Penn State University as a mechanical engineering major. Penn State encouraged cooperative learning (known as a co-op) as a way for students to gain practical experience while working for a semester with professionals in their respective fields, so I decided it was time to give the "real world" a shot. With the hope of building my resume, I applied for several co-op positions at large companies. At that point, I didn't fully recognize or appreciate the value of experience; I just wanted a good paying job where I could show people that I was a fast learner and a hard worker. I accepted a co-op with a large chemical company. I chose the program primarily because it was the highest paying of all my offers.

In the winter of 1997, I left Penn State and headed to one of the largest chemical plants in the United States. Instead of spending the semester at school, I was going to earn credits and receive a paycheck. Housing was provided, so I roomed with other students from around the country who were also in co-op programs. It was an exciting venture.

It certainly wasn't my first job, but it was the first time in my employment history where I was required to wear a tie to work. I had no corporate experience, but I wanted to contribute as much as possible. I knew that I might be performing "gofer" duties, but perhaps, if I was lucky, I could work on a few interesting projects with some of the best engineers in the country. For weeks, I woke up in the dark of the midwestern morning and arrived at the office before most of the other employees. I was *ready!* My new boss gave me several small tasks that I hoped were critical to the department, and I was determined not to let him down. By the end of the first few weeks, I had already completed and checked off these relatively simple tasks, one by one. Then I suddenly realized that I had no work to do, so I repeatedly approached my boss and asked if he needed any help.

Light Bulb Moment—Learning How the Corporation Operated

Believe it or not, the boss simply rebuffed my pleas for additional assignments. I asked him again and again, but he continued to ignore me, knowing that I was being paid for doing absolutely nothing. He simply could not be bothered to find me something else to work on. It was at this point I began to suspect that perhaps I did not fit into corporate life.

For my boss, work was something to be avoided. He rolled into the office around nine in the morning and left for home around four in the afternoon, while squeezing in a nap after lunch on most days. In addition to his minimal office hours, I realized that my boss had perfected the science of telling those who reported to him why their ideas simply would not work. He had a real knack for negating *any* idea, no matter how big or small. And if an idea resulted in the possibility that he or anyone on his team might have some additional work on their plate, he would knock it down like a prizefighter. Of course, he also possessed a strong understanding of how the chain of command worked in a corporation. Therefore, if an idea was presented by colleagues in a meeting, he would not squash it with quite the same vigor that he used with me or other underlings, but he nevertheless did his best to gently but firmly resist all attempts at change.

This left me in an awkward position. No new project meant I had nothing to do. I still showed up at seven in the morning and left late at night. What was I doing during those hours? To this day, I am trying to figure it out. I am certain that I brought no value to the company. However, I did increase my understanding of the value of my time. After about a month at the co-op, I approached other department heads, asking if they needed any help. I was able to conjure up a few willing souls to provide me with assignments, as long as I promised that it would not interfere with the "work" I was doing for my boss. Fortunately, I found one manager in particular who valued my enthusiasm and ability to complete tasks in a timely and efficient manner. As he and I spent more time together, I began to understand how big corporations worked. For many people within the corporation, the goal was to avoid making mistakes. People were not rewarded for making great decisions, but they certainly were punished for making bad ones. If you totally avoided decisions, then all was well with the world. This obviously made it difficult to initiate any positive changes within the organization.

Never Met a Meeting They Didn't Like

"Let's have a meeting" was perhaps the most frequently used phrase at my site. Fear of making mistakes led to a basic cover-your-butt culture. This meant that most people in the organization did not feel comfortable making the simplest decision without building a complete and total consensus in a meeting. This mindset led to meetings, plus meetings to prepare for the meetings, and meetings to digest what was discussed at the meetings. It was a common joke that meeting overload was a company-wide problem, but it was an established element of the culture, and while everyone knew it was an inefficient use of time, no one dared break the tradition. Why? Because if you made a decision without allowing others the opportunity to object to that decision and the outcome of the decision proved unfavorable, you were hung out to dry. This abuse of the employees' time led them, in turn, to abuse the company's time.

I doubt my boss started his career by coming in at nine, leaving at four, and snoozing in his office, but over time, like many people, he began to resent the maddening waste of his time. Internally, once he realized the company was wasting his time, he felt no guilt about wasting the company's time.

During my co-op experience, it became clear to me that "politics" ruled the organization. Preference and power were bestowed on those with friends who had moved up the ladder. This was perhaps the most damaging aspect of the company's culture. It created an environment where people felt helpless and hopeless. Their ability to succeed and be rewarded was based not on their merit or how they performed at work, but on their friendships and relationships with people in higher standing. This produced an entirely new dynamic, and the individuals who followed the naked emperor were more likely to be promoted than those who told the emperor that he was naked. As the "politicians" within the corporation were promoted, they in turn promoted their fellow "politicians" until the leadership of the organization was jam-packed with—you guessed it—"politicians." This resulted in an organization with people at the top who were more concerned with rank and appearances than results.

These issues within the corporation led to a culture where employees with an entrepreneurial streak either left the company or eventually had their enthusiasm sucked out of them. The few remaining entrepreneurs who stayed at the company simply gave up, adapted to the unspoken rules, and internalized their frustrations. They may not have verbalized it, but I saw it in their joyless faces. To me, they seemed powerless to make decisions, resentful that the company wasted their precious time, and resigned to the fact that the quality of their work was not the determining factor in their ability to advance. I saw little sense of urgency and less ambition. It was downright depressing.

The Bitter Truth

Toward the end of my co-op, I was asked to complete a questionnaire about my experience. As a young idealist, I wanted to be frank with my boss in an attempt to help him if, God forbid, he had another co-op employee. I called my dad, a corporate veteran, and asked him if it was the right thing to do. "Your boss is going to be furious," my dad warned me, but I wrote my forthright evaluation anyway. To avoid the appearance of writing my review behind my boss's back, I decided to share a copy of it with him. Just as my dad had predicted, my boss was not pleased with my feedback. After screaming at me and ranting on about my immaturity, the boss demanded that I change my evaluation to something that was more positive. But I held firm, confident that my rating and comments were accurate. I was not going to change a thing. If the atmosphere at work was stifling before this incident, you can imagine the tension that hung in the air afterward. Several days later, I received my boss's review of my co-op performance. He did not discuss it with me personally; he just dropped it in my mail slot, because at that point he was not even speaking to me. Of course, the evaluation was poor, as I expected.

At that point, I knew for certain that my career at this company would go nowhere, but I did not care. Although I had been quite eager to learn and grow when I entered the co-op program, it only took a few months to convince me that at this company—and probably many other large companies—my fate would be determined by people whose values differed from mine. If I stayed in this type of environment, my own self-worth and happiness would be tied to the "politics" of the company, and my potential for success would be in the hands of others. Worst of all, my success would not be determined by my merit. This was simply unacceptable to me, so I left two weeks before my co-op program officially ended. It was for the best because I was wasting their money, and they were wasting my time.

I do not regret my co-op experience. In fact, I consider it one of my greatest learning experiences. It taught me firsthand about the importance of time. I realized that if an individual and a company value time differently, the situation constantly strains their relationship and fails to optimize their needs. (There will be more on the topic of time in chapter 13.)

Most of all, my co-op experience helped me realize that I was best suited for a much more entrepreneurial environment, one in which hard work and justified risk taking are encouraged and rewarded. The three and a half months I spent in the program were critical to creating who I am and what I believe in.

Thankfully, by the time I founded Mitos four years after my co-op experience, I had been exposed to other corporate cultures that were much more positive and effective. These businesses helped me recognize that we needed to sow innovation into Mitos' culture from day one. We accomplished this at Mitos by rewarding successful, calculated risk taking, and treating failures as learning steps in the creative process. We allowed people to make mistakes and did not punish them for those mistakes, which in turn allowed me to make mistakes without judgment from my team.

Risky Business

When I set out to build Mitos I knew that the marketplace we were entering required innovation, and, as a company, we were determined to build that into our culture. This is often easier said than done, and, of course, our actions had to speak louder than our words.

In the spring of 2004 I purchased all of the outstanding shares of I-4, a company that five individuals and I had founded two years earlier, and meshed it into the Mitos group of companies. The business had been successful, yet it was not optimizing its position in the marketplace. Among other challenges, I-4 manufactured silicone gaskets with a very specific use in the biotech industry. Although the product had a competitive advantage over the market alternative, the sales growth of this product was limited because it lacked an effective distribution channel, and we felt that our established means of distribution at Mitos would enable the business to grow more quickly.

After the acquisition of I-4, I challenged Karen Meadows, our head of marketing at Mitos, to develop a sales campaign that would encourage market awareness of the product. As always, I requested that she do so with a minimal budget, especially since we had spent most of our free cash flow purchasing I-4. Karen came back with an innovative plan that entailed custom-made chocolate gaskets to give to customers at trade shows. The marketing plan was clever, but because chocolate gaskets turned out to be quite expensive—costlier than making silicone gaskets, in fact!—it went well above our original budget. However, the campaign was so clever and original that I approved the plan. How did the chocolate gasket marketing campaign fare? Well, although customers thought it was a fantastic idea, the edible keepsakes yielded almost no results and did nothing to demonstrate our competitive advantage. It was certainly disappointing, and we quickly learned that "cute" did not necessarily translate into sales. Some organizations may have reprimanded Karen for spending literally the entire year's marketing budget on a plan that delivered nothing. But that was not part of our culture. We all took a risk, it did not pay off, but we learned from it.

But the story doesn't stop there. In 2005, Karen took the lessons from that marketing endeavor and tried a different approach. She started by asking our team to verbalize our competitive advantage in the field. We all concluded that our company's strong points were the diversity of our product line and the ability to offer our customers complete systems. Karen digested this fact and later devised an interesting marketing idea: the creation of a scavenger hunt at our largest industry trade show. Prior to the trade show, we mailed game cards with clues to many customers and potential clients. The scavenger hunt was interactive, requiring customers to visit the booths of our partners and suppliers. Along the way, these customers learned plenty about who we were and what we could do for them. The game created a buzz among visitors to the trade show who wanted to join in the fun. At the end of the trade show, there was no doubt about it: the scavenger hunt was spectacular, and our sales began to skyrocket immediately. The key to this tale is that we were open to a terrific marketing plan because of a company culture that did not punish unsuccessful risk taking.

Where Merit Is Due

The lessons learned in my co-op experience stayed with me. When we first started Mitos, I was determined—above all else—to create a meritocracy, a culture in which individuals were rewarded and promoted on their performance, not on who they knew or with whom they had lunch. I strongly felt that antimeritocracy sentiments diminished a company by placing less qualified people in leadership positions and demotivating the entire organization. My co-op experience certainly taught me that much.

Here's an unusual example of meritocracy. In the summer of 2004, while I was in the Philadelphia airport waiting for a flight, I stood in line to order a piece of pizza for lunch. The line was moving very slowly, and as I inched closer to the counter, I realized that, while three people were on duty at the pizza establishment, only one person was actually working. And he was working hard, cooking the pizza, preparing the drinks, and ringing up the sales, while the two other "workers" just sat there and chatted with each other, occasionally helping out when they felt like it. I was impressed with the fellow's industry, especially compared to the other pizza employees. When I paid for my lunch, I gave the hard-working man my business card and asked him to call me if he was interested in working for our company. He nodded politely and said thank you in an accent that I barely understood. The next day, I received a call from Sibri, the no-nonsense pizza employee. Although it was difficult to decipher his heavily accented English, we managed to communicate, and the next day he arrived at Mitos for an interview. We learned that Sibri was a political refugee from Togo, West Africa, who had arrived in the United States six months earlier. English was his fourth language. We were impressed by his energy and hired him for a shipping-and-receiving position in our warehouse. Over the next three years, Sibri mastered the English language and eventually earned a master's degree in business. He became a top performer at Mitos, working hard and inspiring his colleagues to work harder. He was entrepreneurial minded, an individual who saw opportunity where others only saw problems, a natural leader to whom others were drawn. Sibri was regularly promoted, and after several years, he was named an operations leader with multiple shifts reporting to him. There were other staff members who had more experience and education than Sibri, but he earned additional responsibility and was rewarded solely because of his merit.

Respect of Time

At Mitos we created a culture that was not only a meritocracy, but one in which the individual's time was valued. This, in turn, led to an environment where individuals valued the company's time and resources. Our team of employees "went the extra mile" when needed because they respected the organization and understood that the organization respected them.

This came in handy in the spring of 2006, when we were literally selling a product as fast as we could produce it. In the midst of our overwhelming workload, several big orders arrived unexpectedly. We could have declined to take those orders, but we knew that we were embedded into this customer's overall manufacturing process, and they *needed* us to deliver. So we ditched Plan A *and* Plan B and devised what we called "Plan C." We sat down as a team and laid out the facts. In essence, we needed to immediately double production, even though we were already at 100 percent capacity. We developed a plan whereby every person in the company contributed to the product-manufacturing department, and the manufacturing division committed to substantial overtime. We also rented additional space nearby to store raw materials. Michael Ryan, our head of engineering, quickly took an active operations role to help oversee all of the products. The plan was neither perfect nor problem-free, but in the end, we met our customer's demands. The main reason we made the deadline was because we were a team built on mutual respect. Our organization never wasted anyone's time, so when the organization asked for more time from individuals, it was returned without exception or reprisal.

Culture is insidious and difficult to quantify. Maybe that's why, in today's matrix-driven culture, so few companies understand and focus on its importance. An entrepreneurial organization's culture, driven from the top down, requires a firm commitment to think on a long-term time scale and value everyone's contribution to a company.

What you should know:

- *Innovation must be sown into the company culture. This happens by rewarding successful risk taking and treating failures as part of the creative process.*

- *People often spend more time at work than anywhere else, including home, so it is critical that your ability and time are respected at work. This has a tremendous impact on your feeling of self-worth.*
- *Build a culture rooted in trust and respect, from the president to the janitor.*
- *Culture will contribute to success more than anything else. People will come and go in an organization. Market trends will force companies to adapt and change paths. That adaption is made easier with a strong culture seeped in innovation, meritocracy, and respect.*

Six

Positive Atmosphere

Culture embodies a company's value system; it is how people within an organization operate at all times, even when no one is watching. Culture is the soul of a company. If it was the co-op project that taught me how culture could damage a company, it was W. L. Gore & Associates that taught me how culture could elevate a company and its people.

Decisions, Decisions

The summer before I started my freshman year of college, I wanted to make as much money as possible so that I did not have to work part time while at school. My brother used some contacts he had to land me an interview for an assembly line job at W. L. Gore & Associates in Newark, Delaware. It was a third-shift position, which meant I worked from 10 p.m. to 6 a.m. At the time, Gore had about 6,000 employees and manufactured a plethora of well-known consumer products, including Gore-Tex® fabrics and Glide® dental floss. My role that summer was in the less glamorous electronic products division, which manufactured many of the behind-the-scenes products used in consumer computers and electronics.

My summer at Gore was rough because I never fully adapted to sleeping during the day, which meant I hardly slept all summer. The assembly-line job was tremendously repetitious, and that, combined with severe sleep-deprivation, made it difficult to keep my mind focused on the task at hand. Nevertheless, I did my job and also took mental notes of my workplace. By the end of the summer, while I certainly learned a great deal of practical information about how a manufacturing plant operates, I was also deeply impressed with the dedication of the Gore employees with whom I worked. The people at Gore taught me that a quality staff is what makes the difference between an organization's success or failure. My coworkers at Gore—most of them single mothers—chose to work the "graveyard shift" so that they could be home during the day when their children woke up and when they returned from school. Perhaps it was the circumstances of our personal lives that motivated us through those long nights, but we definitely formed a close-knit community on the third shift. Despite the grueling toll of working through the night, the atmosphere was upbeat, positive, and all-inclusive. I soon realized that no matter what your position was at Gore, you were free to share ideas with colleagues or with upper management. The assembly-line workers in my division were aware of their contributions to the company and truly cared about its success. It was an inviting, democratic environment that, even as an eighteen-year-old, I recognized as something special.

Four years later, in 1999, I graduated with a mechanical engineering degree from Penn State. At that time, the economy was booming, so even before I walked away with my diploma, I had three job offers from Standard & Poor's 500 companies. In addition to these bright prospects, I was also offered a position at my "alma mater," Gore.

I remembered from my summer on the assembly line that Gore truly had a unique culture. Even as a third-shift temporary worker, I knew that Gore's mission was based on innovation, a flat structure (as opposed to a pyramid-shaped hierarchy), and an active interest in developing and nurturing each employee's skills. Because of these unique characteristics, Gore seemed like a perfect fit for me and was undoubtedly my first choice as a work destination, but there was a catch: the salary was 25 percent below the offers I had received from other companies. This was a crucial caveat because my main goal as a broke college graduate was to save money for my future, whether that included a house or perhaps even a business of my own. As I ruminated over my dilemma and compared possible annual salaries, I flashed back several years to the time I selected the co-op project mainly because it paid the most. If my co-op experience taught me one thing, it was that money doesn't mean anything if you land in the middle of a nightmare. With that in mind, I turned down the higher offers and chose Gore. In my heart I was convinced that I would learn a great deal there and fit more comfortably into their uniquely collaborative environment. (I like to think that this was the third best decision in my life, after marriage and Mitos.)

After I was hired and became engulfed in the culture at Gore, it was clear that I had definitely made the right choice of workplace. To put it simply, Gore was basically the opposite of my previous experience at a large company. In contrast to the disengaged staff at the chemical company, the Gore employees were passionate about their company. Gore's culture and its business success are so outstanding that there have been entire books dedicated to examining the company and its philosophy. Without diminishing the volumes of work by others, I believe that Gore's culture can be summed up in one word: *respect.*

In the Beginning ...

When Bill Gore founded W.L. Gore & Associates in 1958, his goal was not only to create a product, but a company rooted in respect. Prior to founding his business, Bill was a research and development chemist at DuPont. One night, in a basement lab that he had set up in his home, he uncovered a method for making computer ribbon cable insulation. Excited about his discovery, Bill took the idea to his colleagues at DuPont, but they weren't interested, so he decided to head back to his basement and start his own company. It was literally a mom-and-pop operation, with employees living at the Gore house and Bill's wife involved in building the business.

By 1971, Bill and his son Robert discovered the infamous product known as Gore-Tex, which remains the company's flagship technology. As his company flourished, Bill vowed to avoid the hierarchical structure that burdened many large corporations and create a business devoid of ranks or titles. At Gore, every employee was deemed an "associate," and no one was hired unless a company associate agreed to sponsor the person and mentor him or her. Also, to foster communication and camaraderie, Bill felt that employees should work in small, autonomous divisions. He also stressed innovation, creativity, collaboration, and energy—an environment in which he himself thrived.

To reinforce his goal of creating an atmosphere where people were genuinely passionate about their work and about the company, Bill eventually turned Gore into an Employee Stock Ownership Plan (ESOP). This means that the company is owned by the employees. In their ESOP, Gore employees receive 15 percent of their salary in company stock, which is vested over five years and held until retirement. For most employees, the ESOP is their primary source of retirement funds. Once they retire, Gore employees sell their shares back to the company based on a price that is evaluated quarterly by an outside service. Although the Gore family probably remains the largest individual owner of the firm, every Gore employee performs and makes decisions as a part-owner of the company. This group ownership reinforces a culture of respect that I have rarely seen duplicated. Of course, if you stroll through any Gore facility, you won't see the word *respect* carved into a marble cornerstone or mentioned in memos, but Gore's culture is nevertheless deeply rooted in respect for the company and individuals' respect for each other.

A Proud Legacy

Bill Gore passed in 1986, but he would be proud that his distinctive corporate culture has survived and prospered. Although he started from the ground up—literally, in his basement—Bill's company is now considered one of the most innovative in the world, with about $2 billion in annual revenues and 7,500 employees who work on more than a thousand products, from filters for reducing air pollution to guitar strings. A company owner must possess an element of unselfishness in order to turn his or her company into an

ESOP, and Bill had the foresight and courage to do so. An owner must be willing to depart with equity (ownership) and trust that the individuals receiving the ownership will nurture the business in the manner in which it was originally intended. As evidenced at Gore, an ESOP represents a show of respect from the owner to the employees, and, in turn, it enables employees to respect the owner.

Think about it this way: Have you ever rented a car? If so—even if you are an extremely responsible person—you probably filled the rental vehicle with a lower grade of gasoline or drove it a little harder than your own beloved auto. The same is true of companies. Company owners take better care of a business than people who do not have ownership in the company. Employee Stock Ownership Plans create an environment where everyone owns a stake in the company and, as a result, inspire everyone to respect the company. The ESOP empowers individuals, from the CEO to the shop floor worker, to perform thoughtfully and intelligently, and to do what is best for the company long term. When an employee is a company owner, the goal is not instant gratification, but future value creation, that is, the future value of a business's stock. Future value creation is important to employees in an ESOP company because they own stock which they will "cash in" twenty years down the road upon retirement. They are invested in a company that will benefit them only if it endures. This knowledge, I have observed, creates a very different mindset than that in publicly traded companies (which will be discussed later).

At Gore, the prevailing atmosphere of respect ultimately led to trust. The trust allowed the organization to operate in an efficient manner that could not be achieved in a culture that lacked respect. It empowered people to make decisions. It created an environment where calculated risk taking was acceptable, which allowed innovations to progress. When I compare Gore to other companies, one of the biggest differences is that at Gore, employees simply did not fear taking risks and/or making mistakes. During my co-op experience, I saw how fear of making mistakes led to tremendous inefficiencies when many people were brought into every decision, no matter how minor. For example, when a dozen people endure ten two-hour meetings to decide whose responsibility it is to answer the phones when the receptionist is at lunch, a company begins to drown in the inertia of cumbersome waste. Although this example sounds a bit exaggerated, I have witnessed companies in which it took 200 people-hours to decide the most basic, nitpicky issues. Obviously, in most businesses, key matters require meetings and thoughtful input from appropriate staff members, but balance and common sense should prevail in decision making. Companies with cultures rooted in respect, including ESOPs, are inspired to find this balance.

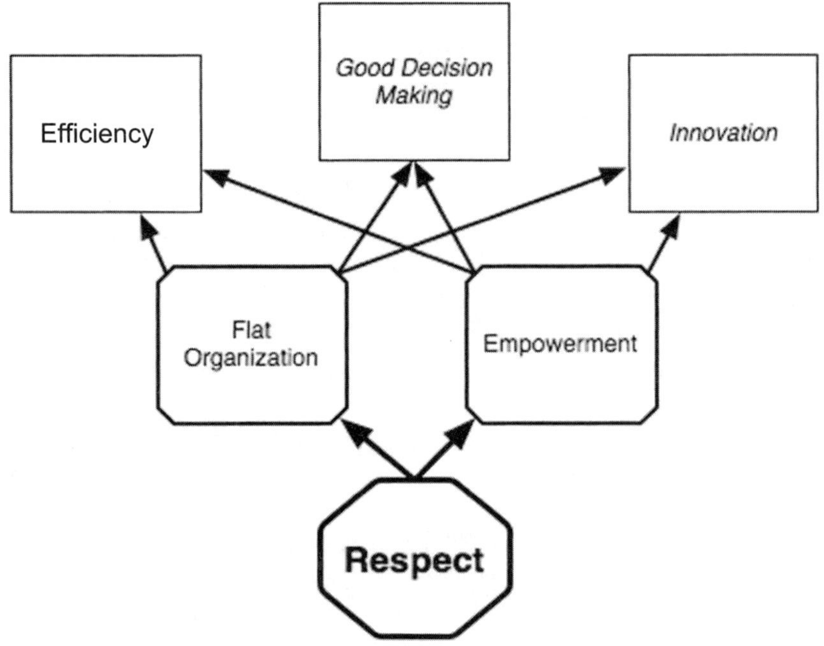

Keeping It Small

At Gore, respecting the individual allowed the company to decentralize, which in turn empowered the employees. In 2000, although Gore had roughly 6,000 employees, its structure was very unique for an organization of that size. For example, each facility within the Gore organization had teams of no more than 200 people (what other companies often referred to as "business units"), each with a clear leader. Leaders within Gore did not make decisions in a vacuum; instead, all decisions were determined by those employees closest to the issues. This allowed the company to benefit from the advantages of a large-scale organization—such as purchasing power—while maintaining the nimbleness of a smaller, more agile start-up. The structure wisely enabled those closest to the opportunity or the issues to make decisions.

After all, who is more qualified to be involved in business decisions than those people affected by the topic, day in and day out? This sounds perfectly logical, yet I am amazed by how often large organizations make decisions from the top down, with little or no input from those who are most familiar with the subject. Think of a major sales decision made by a company vice president without even consulting the sales force. That is as ridiculous as it is inefficient. Gore's employees are empowered and, as a result, allocate resources more efficiently than companies whose employees are encumbered. Innovation is easier when it is driven by those closest to the customer. The best ideas typically spring from those who have needs, that is, customers. Gore's flat organizational structure, coupled with the respect of individuals toward each other, allowed people closest to the customers to prioritize and make decisions. This freedom and belief in an employee's good judgment ultimately led to Gore innovations that enjoyed a high success rate.

Many People, One Goal

Of course, Gore was not Shangri-La, so I found that some politics existed within the organization, but it was very limited. Bickering and backstabbing were rare because there was a sense of community, a feeling of belonging and purpose that inspired individuals to believe in the company culture. As owners, the ultimate goal of Gore employees was to develop a long-lasting, prosperous company. I suspect that the individuals who did not believe in the culture ultimately did not succeed and left the company. This created a natural selection process and an ongoing flow of positive energy that continually reinforced the Gore culture.

Some large companies offer stock options and various incentives tied to performance, but these do not match the impact made by an ESOP. I believe that Gore's ESOP worked so well because:

(1) Every employee in the company was involved in the plan, so it reinforced the idea of respect at all levels.

(2) It was sustainable. Fifteen percent of a person's salary grabs *everyone's* attention.

(3) Shares were not redeemed until the individual retired, which caused employees to focus on long-term value creation as opposed to inflating current stock prices.

Other companies offer only to their leaders enormous incentives and stock options that exceed 15 percent while simultaneously offering lower-level employees incentives below 15 percent. This discrepancy creates an environment that builds barriers between various levels within the company and inspires varying degrees of motivation. The beauty behind the Gore plan was that its uniform 15 percent policy united everyone in the company, no matter the capacity in which they worked.

A Stitch in Time

In 1850, it took Isaac Singer $40 and 11 days to improve upon a previous invention known as the sewing machine. The earlier sewing machine incarnations were difficult to produce and awkward to use. Singer's invention, which used a straight eye needle, was the world's first practical version of a sewing machine. It exploded into a blockbuster success. Within ten years, Singer expanded his sewing machine production into a global company and took home the prestigious first prize at the 1855 World's Fair in Paris. By 1880, the company was selling over 500,000 machines each year, capturing an astonishing 90 percent of the worldwide sewing machine market. By 1913, the company was selling 3,000,000 units annually, and its headquarters were located in the world's tallest building (when it was built in 1908), the Singer Building on Broadway and Liberty Street in New York City.

Prior to Singer's invention, people around the globe hand-sewed everything from bedding to sails to clothing. Sewing was considered a basic yet vitally important skill, but Singer's new sewing machine changed the manner in which the world sewed. Like many great inventions, the machine produced many positive social implications. For the first time in history, instead of hand-tailoring an item of clothing, standardized garments were efficiently and inexpensively manufactured en masse. In many ways, the ability to mass-produce clothing with the sewing machine marked the beginning of the fashion industry. When the cost of making clothing plummeted worldwide, it helped to increase the general standard of living. Even people with meager resources could, for the first time, afford to clothe themselves and still have money to spend on items that were previously viewed as luxuries.

In the tradition of many great start-up companies, Singer's sewing machine created a wave of new technologies and needs in the marketplace. Due to the sheer volume of new sewing machines, businesses designed to service and repair the machines quickly mushroomed. To meet the incredible demand for sewing machines, worldwide sales, distribution, and manufacturing rapidly evolved. In addition to his technological skills, Singer was also a creative marketer who developed the first form of modern-day financing, allowing individuals to purchase a sewing machine on an installment plan. This ability to bring automated sewing machines into private homes dramatically increased the efficiency of households and allowed families time for other matters, including leisure activities. Owning a sewing machine became a huge status symbol and a "must have" in most middle-class homes.

NewAge for New Ideas

In 1951, almost a century after Isaac Singer introduced the world to his discovery, Raymond Baker started working for the Singer Corporation. At the time, the company had roughly $300,000,000 in annual sales and employed over 100,000 people. Nevertheless, Raymond soon discovered that the glory years of the sewing machine industry were ending. He also felt strongly that he didn't really fit into the corporate environment. So after a brief but successful career at Singer, Raymond left the organization to join a start-up company called NewAge International.

NewAge, which distributed testing equipment, was founded by an Englishman who had taken his firm overseas and entered the American market. As one of NewAge's first six employees in the United States, Raymond quickly realized that the New York company was poorly managed and losing money hand over fist. Less than a year after he joined the company, Raymond was unemployed because NewAge shut down. The father of four young children decided that NewAge International was a solid business idea that had crumbled due to poor management, so he flew to England and asked the owner if he could purchase the business. With a loan from NewAge's owner, Raymond bought the company and moved it from New York to the Philadelphia suburbs.

That gutsy move began a long but passionate journey for Raymond and his family. Ken Baker, Raymond's son and currently the CEO of NewAge Industries, reflects on the company's history with great pride. His favorite memory is a 1953 photo of his parents wearing rubber boots, pouring concrete for the floor of the company's new building. Unfortunately, although the entire family worked hard to help build the new structure, it was completely demolished by the fury of Hurricane Hazel in 1954. Like all successful entrepreneurs, however, Raymond did not let this unexpected natural disaster abort his business dream, and he soon rebuilt the facility.

As the business sprouted, Raymond decided to purchase a large, run-down facility in the Philadelphia suburb of Willow Grove, Pennsylvania. Ken remembers the days when his entire family pitched in and participated in the renovations. They set up a kitchen in the building, and Ken's mother cooked all of the family's meals there so that they wasted no time traveling back and fourth from their house to eat. At the time, Ken was a young boy. and his job was straightening nails (one of Raymond's creative means of reducing costs during the renovation). When an old wall was torn down, it was Ken's duty to remove and straighten any nails that remained so that the nails could be reused to manufacture a new wall.

Ken's days of straightening nails are behind him, but his memories of the sacrifices that he and the rest of his family made remain with him. His father, Raymond, is still involved in the business; but as CEO, it was Ken's decision to transform the company into an ESOP. Ken's idea for employee-ownership first took hold in the early 1990s when Total Quality Management

(TQM) was sweeping the country. NewAge hired TQM consultants to transform their quality system. As Ken reviewed the consultants' suggestions regarding work flow and quality control, it struck him that while it was an improvement, the only way to truly enhance the system was if every employee viewed the company and its products from the same perspective that he did. In his gut, Ken knew that for a quality management plan to ultimately prove effective, employees had to embrace it as owners of the company. In the decade following his hypothesis, Ken learned about several different types of ownership structures, but decided that an ESOP would prove most successful at NewAge.

In 2000, Ken devised a process that eventually transitioned his family's business to an ESOP by 2006. The NewAge marketing literature reads: "Employee-owned for your benefit." The ESOP has only been in place for about two years, but you can practically feel how proud Ken is that NewAge made the shift. The results of becoming an ESOP, he says, are already clearly noticeable, and "people are just more engaged in the business." Ken is passionate about NewAge, and, I would guess, he finds purpose in providing an atmosphere in which people enjoy working. While Ken no longer needs to work to survive, he can still be found at the office or with a customer almost every day.

When I owned Mitos, NewAge was a supplier as well as a competitor, so I know their business well. NewAge might not be as widely recognized as Gore, but their experience with ESOPs is very similar. Both are offshoots of large organizations. Both firms have an underlining mantra of respect that enables them to outperform many of their competitors. They also have employees at all levels who are engaged in decision-making processes and who truly care about their customers and their company's sustainability.

As I examine different company structures, it is clear that the most effective are those where everyone is engaged in long-term value creation.

On Purpose

Culture is the soul of a company that guides interaction and behavior. Purpose is the main reason *why* the company exists. Like culture, a company's purpose looms larger than any individual. Purpose represents our natural connectivity with one another, and, as many psychological studies have shown, everyone needs a purpose in his or her life. Many people achieve a sense of purpose outside of their job; however, when you find purpose within your work environment, you really hit the jackpot! All successful companies have a purpose, or they do not survive. That is why it is critical to communicate this purpose to employees so that they fully understand how the business benefits society. Once they recognize the company's purpose, employees are more likely to be motivated to succeed and grow as a team. Have you ever worked at a pointless job that you absolutely detested? Then you know just how much more enjoyable it is to wake up every morning, happy to begin your day, excited about working for a company that adds value to society.

The Need for Nurses

In 1973, Mark Baiada had a meeting with himself. The twenty-five-year-old business graduate was the son of hard-working immigrant parents (his father from Sicily and his mother from Yugoslavia). Mark grew up in a family of self-employed individuals. His father ran his own insurance company, and an uncle was a serial entrepreneur involved in everything from service businesses to manufacturing. Mark was inspired by these role models from an early age and decided that he wanted to run his own business someday. However, at age twenty-five, he felt like he was falling behind in getting to where he wanted in life, so he recommitted himself to moving forward and starting his own business. He also developed a personal plan in which he dedicated himself to becoming a student of American business. (Personal plans will be further discussed in chapter 12.) He began studying financial sheets, reading the business section of the newspaper, and talking to anyone he could find who ran his or her own business.

With $16,000 of his own savings in hand, Mark knew that he wanted to create a business that was not only successful but also socially responsible and scalable from coast to coast. Most importantly, he had already learned that a rising tide lifts all boats and was looking for an industry with long-term growth.

After two years of searching, Mark came across a home health care business model idea that fit his long-term goal. The macro trends in the home health field were undeniable: there was a need, and it would continue as the population aged. While he planned to start his home health care venture in Philadelphia, he was confident that he could expand the model nationwide. In addition, he was satisfied that the idea for his business brought tremendous value to society.

Care Across the Country

Today, Bayada Nurses employs 14,000 people and annually generates half a billion dollars in revenue. For the last thirty years, Mark built his dream, and today his organization clearly outperforms its peers. When I asked Mark why Bayada was the industry leader, he reached into his pocket and pulled out a small 3″ × 6″ trifold card on high quality stock. With pride, he explained that every employee within the organization carries one of these cards on his or her person at all times. As I glanced at the card, I saw three large words, "The Bayada Way," and a list of the company's mission, beliefs, and values.

Embedded in the company mission statement is its core purpose: "Bayada Nurses have a special purpose—to help people have a safe home life with comfort, independence, and dignity. Bayada Nurses provides skilled, rehabilitative, therapeutic and personal home health care services to children, adults and seniors nationwide. We care for our clients 24 hours a day, seven days a week. Families coping with significant illness or disability need help and support while caring for a family member. Our goal at Bayada Nurses is to provide the highest quality home care service available. We believe our clients and their families deserve home health care delivered with *compassion, excellence and reliability,* our Bayada Nurses' core values."[8]

The Bayada mission brings purpose to the care that is provided each and every day by its employees. While there is no empirical evidence to which Mark can point to, he is confident that his employee turnover is lower than that of his

---

[8] Bayda Nurses Home Care Specialists, "Bayda Nurse's Mission Statement,",http://www.bayada.com/mission.shtml

competitors. I suspect that his employees are more satisfied with their jobs; after all, the value that they bring to the world around them is apparent. In Mark's mind, this is one of the key reasons that his organization has been able to grow so quickly. He and his team are committed to a purpose larger than any individual.

Despite Mark's incredible achievement, his company headquarters consists of a small, one-story building housing five administrative employees. In addition, he has accomplished the growth of his organization without taking on any outside investors or a cent of debt. It is obvious that Mark's down-to-earth leadership and unpretentiousness helped the company grow from a single employee taking care of a handful of clients to about 14,000 employees who help hundreds of thousands of people live a better life.

Bayada Nurses has competitors who provide the same types of services; however, none seem to have grown to Bayada's stature with as little capital. Why? Mark understands the purpose of the company, and, just as importantly, he clearly articulates this purpose to the company's employees. By embedding this purpose in everyone, he provides a framework in which the company can grow more efficiently than a company that does not provide this message. At Bayada Nurses, everyone is cognizant of the purpose of the business, and with this unified philosophy, decisions are made by individuals at all levels within the organization. Most importantly, employees at all levels are more satisfied with their jobs because they understand the value that they bring to the world around them. This decreases employee turnover and increases job performance, both of which lead to increased value creation.

But don't mistake purpose with altruism. For example, a trash-removal business does not appear nearly as benevolent as an altruistic organization like the Red Cross, yet it still has a purpose: keeping neighborhoods clean. I have been to Naples, a once beautiful city that now allows trash to pile up in its neighborhoods. The debris is unsanitary and unsightly, and has sent the city into a downward spiral. The situation in Naples illustrates how much every job within society *matters*. Trash-removal business owners who fully understand the critical purpose of their company and communicate it to their team will be more successful than trash-removal companies that go through the motions of half-heartedly collecting rubbish.

Companies that possess a strong culture rooted in respect with a clearly defined purpose benefit the entire ecosystem that surrounds the business, including employees, customers, and suppliers.

What you should know:

- *Create a culture of respect; this enables the organization to operate more efficiently and benefits all stakeholders in the long run.*
- *Create a structure that empowers people; this is the only way an organization can grow quickly and efficiently.*
- *Provide a mechanism for employees within your organization to own part of the company.*
- *Develop and communicate your purpose, internally and externally.*

Seven

By All Means, Value Your Company's Value

I am an engineer, and, like most engineers, I love neat ideas: how things work, why they work, and how to make them work better are all irresistible topics for the engineering mind.

Entrepreneurs are another group that gobble up new ideas like candy. Unfortunately, this passion for fascinating ideas has a tendency to land entrepreneurs in trouble. They often become so overexcited about an idea that they fail to recognize whether or not it can evolve into a viable business venture. To objectively decide if a business idea has "legs," I believe that the fundamental question to ask is: does this product or service bring value to society? While I recognize that this sounds overly dramatic, it is the fundamental question to which all great companies can answer yes.

In the long run, a business must generate at least a break-even cash flow to survive. You may have the greatest intentions in the world to build a business that will contribute to society, but if a company fails to meet its expenses—including paying its employees—it will also fail to meet its well-intentioned goals. Focusing on value allows entrepreneurs to determine if an idea is viable.

The Iridium Example

In November 1998, then–Vice President of the United States Al Gore made the first call on a cell phone designed by the Iridium communications service. After more than a decade in the making and $6 billion in start-up costs, the Iridium network of communication satellites was off the ground. The Iridium system was designed to use a network of low earth-orbiting satellites to transmit voices across the planet, from pole to pole. Engineers at Motorola first developed the technology in 1987, and by the mid-1990s, the company planned a commercial use for their technology. At the time, cell phone sales were quickly expanding, but it was still a growing field and not yet a well-established global market.

I still remember hearing about the product for the first time and marveling at its concept. As a person who is drawn to innovation and technology, I instantly fell in love with the idea. But that love was short lived. Less than a year after Al Gore made his famous call, Iridium went bankrupt. What happened? My guess is that the company's leaders fell in love with the concept as well. While their idea was certainly neater than the options their competitors were pursuing, Iridium possessed several shortcomings that should have been identified early on:

1) The technology did not allow the phones to work without a line of sight, which meant it did not work indoors. Even in the mid-1990s, it was clear that cell phones were evolving to a point where people wanted to use them inside of homes and workplaces.

2) The Iridium technology prevented the company from making compact versions of the product. This mistake is probably forgivable because, at the time, most cell phone were also rather large and clumsy. However, it quickly became clear that the technology faced size limitations.

3) The start-up and operational costs were astronomical (estimated at $6 billion), which meant that the consumer's cost was also extremely high. Ironically, when Iridium was introduced, the cost of competitive alternatives was plummeting.

"It was a technology that didn't live up to its hype or its billing," said James Grant, editor of *Grant's Interest Rate Observer,* who has chronicled Iridium's problems, including its limited signal range. "People chose to overlook the risks because they were bedazzled by the technology and the promoters or sponsors." In hindsight, many people saw flaws that the Iridium team failed to recognize. "Everyone in the industry has looked at Iridium as the pioneers of satellite phone service, " said Rikki Lee, editor of *Wireless Week.* "And when they couldn't find anyone to pay $3,000 for a phone and $7 a minute for service, it was like—duh! There aren't all that many people who trek up to the North Pole." [9]

So the answer to the question, "Why did Iridium fail?" is this: it was incredibly expensive to use and designed with inferior technology. In essence, when compared to their competitive alternatives, the cost of the cell phones did not bring proportional value to society.

Placing Value on Your Business's Value

While this concept sounds simplistic, I consider it the number-one source of failure among first-time entrepreneurs. Therefore, I strongly believe that before early stage business owners face the inevitable mountain of challenges to their venture, they should define their fundamental concept and complete the end of this sentence: "Our business brings value to society by __________." The value a product brings to society may be obvious, like a new hospital that promotes wellness in a region that has traditionally been underserved by healthcare institutions, or it may be more subtle, like a board game that brings great joy to the people who play it.

At Mitos, our fundamental business concept was to lower our customers' manufacturing costs. We developed goods and services that enabled the biotech industry to reduce the cost of manufacturing biologic drugs and vaccines, including the flu vaccine. As we built our business, if someone asked us to define Mitos' concept, every single person in our organization knew the answer to that question: to help lower the costs of

---

[9] David Barboza, "Iridium, Bankrupt, Is Planning a Fiery Ending for Its 88 Satellites ," New York Times, April 11, 2000, Technology section.

manufacturing biological drugs and vaccines, and pass those savings on to consumers. The understanding of our company's value allowed us to not only effectively price products that were beneficial to our customers, but also to generate income for our survival and our investment in the future. Just as important, the value to society that our company provided imbued everyone in our organization with a solid sense of purpose. When you are working long hours, sweating through a boatload of crises, and wondering if your business will survive, that purpose means a great deal, not only to you but also to those who are working alongside you. Look at it this way: if you are asked to work eighty hours a week to build a business that produces cigarettes, you probably won't have the same commitment to your task as a person who is building a children's health clinic in a poor neighborhood.

In the Market for Entrepreneurs

In addition to building a business that serves a purpose, it's also wise for entrepreneurs to choose a field that is more prone to success for start-ups. You may have noticed that there are certain markets that tend to attract a greater number of start-ups, and, at least initially, the rates of success increase dramatically in these markets. For example, if you had the choice of starting a business in newspapers or in digital media, which area would you select? Newspapers have existed in some form or another for centuries and historically generated billions of dollars in annual revenue, yet you probably selected digital media. Why? One of the most remarkable things about technology is how each new invention creates both the need for, and possibility of, more inventions.[10] Simply put, newspapers represent a mature industry that has made few changes during the last several decades, with minimal technological advances or innovations to propel it in a new direction. Basically, newspaper trends that were in place thirty years ago remain today. This immobility within the newspaper business has led to established infrastructures that, like poured concrete, have settled over time and are difficult to change. Time has also

---

[10] E. Beinhocker, *The Origin of Wealth* (Boston, MA: Harvard Business School Press, 2006), 246.

turned most newspaper services that were once considered valuable into commodities. A "breaking" frontpage print story once deemed "hot off the presses" is now seen as old news that has already been covered for many hours by Internet sites. In addition, massive consolidation within the newspaper business has divvied most of the industry's power among only a handful of players.

On the other hand, digital media is a young incarnation of the news business that is currently reflected in a scattered and inefficient market. To date, no single player has made a significant impact in the digital industry. Most importantly, innovation rules the day in digital media, which forces the market to change rapidly. This evolution of a fresh market is what creates new needs and opportunities. Start-ups can succeed in any market, but the chance of triumph increases greatly in developing markets. As an entrepreneur, it's wise to find your way into these frontier areas.

Ride the Waves

Albert Charpentier proudly says that he has had three big successes and two big failures. The oldest of six children, Albert remembers his first entrepreneurial endeavor at the age of eleven, selling Burpee seeds door-to-door. He followed his Burpee seed venture by building a newspaper delivery business, and by the time he was a teenager, he had twenty delivery people working for him. Looking back, these were Albert's practices, the testing ground for his skills. Through these early experiences, Albert developed basic, solid strategic thinking. He tried different tactics and learned what did and did not work, which provided him—even at a base level—with a strong understanding of calculated risk. He also developed self-awareness and confidence, which allowed him to evolve into a strong leader.

When he was twenty-one, Albert remembers telling his girlfriend (who eventually became his wife) that by the age of thirty, he was going to have his own company. Albert had a natural love for business, but decided that to reach his entrepreneurial goal, he needed to develop strong technical skills, and so he enrolled at the University of Pennsylvania's

School of Electrical Engineering. After graduating from Penn in 1974, Albert ignored the lure of earning a tidy salary with a large corporation and instead selected a job at MOS Technologies, a four-year-old start-up that was entering the new calculator chip market. He felt that joining a small organization could provide him with the experience he needed for his long-term goal of starting his own company. At the time, the calculator chip market was at its infancy, and chips were literally hand-cut. (Today, thousands of chips are made per hour in a completely automated process.) MOS showed some early success and was acquired by Commodore in 1977.

Following the acquisition, the perpetual entrepreneur Albert made a proposal to the infamous Commodore CEO Jack Tremiel to develop the first color graphics video card. Albert saw the future of computers, and it was not limited to being used as a calculator. Through this process, Albert led the development in what ultimately became the Commodore 64, the first computer designed specifically for home use. While working on Commodore 64, he met a young Harvard student named Bill Gates, from whom the company purchased a software program called BASIC. At the time, Gates was trying to save money to build his business, so he stayed at the home of one of Commodore's engineers instead of a hotel (sacrifice). Commodore paid him $50,000 for the program with no licensing fee, and that was the first and last time Gates ever signed an agreement without such a stipulation. The Commodore 64 was a success, and while Albert had a bright future ahead of him at the company, he stayed true to his word and three weeks before his thirtieth birthday, he left the company to pursue his own venture. Albert had two young children and only a year's worth of savings, but he had set a goal, laid out the intermediate steps, and did everything in his power to meet that goal.

The Games We Play

In 1982, Atari had 1.6 million game units in the field. Although the gaming market was well established, Albert and his team saw the potential to turn these existing machines into more than just game consoles. So he and the two others who joined his start-up developed an add-on device that converted the Atari into a computer. In September of 1982 they began building a prototype; by March 1983, they had sold the company to Atari for $3 million. They did not intend to sell the business, but when the opportunity presented itself, they took the lucrative exit.

After the sale, Albert's days as an entrepreneur continued. He and his two partners reinvested their profits in a new idea: the first multimedia machine for home use. Obviously, this was an enormous undertaking, so Albert and his partners decided to raise outside funds for their company. With an experienced and proven team, they quickly received a term sheet from Kleiner and Perkins, one of the most established and respected venture capital firms in the market. However, 1983 was not a good year for the computer market, and Kleiner eventually decided that a small company could not lead the way in the development of the first home multimedia machine.

Having a term sheet pulled from Kleiner is like being blacklisted during the McCarthy era, and, subsequently, no other venture capital firms even considered investing in the multimedia company. With the development of their new multimedia machine only half completed, Albert and his partners realized that they did not have adequate funds to finish their project. But that did not signal failure to them; it simply meant that they needed to change course. The team evaluated where they were in their process and decided that they could complete the audio chip portion of the product at a relatively low cost. They named the audio chip company Enconiq. After some very basic research, they determined that musicians were innovators who were attracted to new technology. As any 1980s music aficionado knows, electronic keyboards were taking off at the time, but they had limited sound quality and were very expensive.

Music to Their Ears

Albert and his team hired a young MBA graduated named Rob Weber to develop an electric keyboard business and marketing plan for Ensoniq. With a half-million dollars raised, they launched the first electronic keyboard with quality sound that retailed for $1,695. They hired a salesperson and instructed him not to return without a sale because otherwise there was no money to pay him—or anyone else in the company for that matter. By 1985, the company was profitable, with over a million dollars in revenue. Business continued to boom, and they reached $30 million in annual revenue, until 1994, when *MTV Unplugged* signaled the end of the techno years, and sales plummeted 40 percent in one year.

Fortunately, Albert and his team saw the writing on the wall years earlier and had already begun to parlay their music technology into an audio technology company. In 1992, when Microsoft developed audio extensions for Windows, it was Albert's company that was there to sell the audio cards (eight years after they first set out to accomplish this). In 1998, Ensoniq was sold to its largest competitor, Creative Labs, for $84 million. It was the right time to sell. Because innovation was slowing as the product was mass produced, big players were poised to dominate the field and overtake smaller, more innovative companies.

Now Hear This

Albert's path was not without significant detours. In 1988, the company spent millions developing and launching the Sound Selector, the first digital hearing aide. This aide represented an entirely new technology that required a seismic shift of the industry's traditional means of conducting business. While the end user (the person receiving the hearing aide) saw value in the Sound Selector, the individual who Ensoniq needed to target first was the audiologist who "installed" the product for the end user. The Sound Selector required the audiologist to have each patient return several times for adjustments, which was a departure from the existing model in which the audiologist fitted hearing aides for patients in one sitting. Looking back, Albert could have avoided the $8 million that he lost in this project by building an advisory board that truly understood the nuts-and-bolts of the hearing aide market. Twenty years after the launch of Sound Selector, other companies are entering the digital hearing aide market with similar technology, but using a completely different business model that requires a minimal sales force and Internet marketing to balance high customer acquisition costs.

The Right Fit

After selling Ensoniq in 2000, Albert started a company called Intellifit that licensed near-field radar technology. This innovation enabled consumers to use their personalized measurements to purchase appropriately sized clothing online. Once again, there was value to the end user (the person buying the clothes), but before reaching the consumer, the company first had to sell the product to the apparel industry. After almost nine years with the venture, Albert decided it was time to merge Intellifit with Unique Solutions, a Canadian company.

Albert's three successes (Commodore 64, the electronic keyboard, and the audiocard) had two key elements in common: markets that were quickly expanding and the value Albert brought by either offering greater product features/cost reduction. Ultimately, all three possessed significant, definable value to their customers.

Albert's two failures (digital hearing aid and Intellifit) had two key elements in common: they were solid technologies with no viable market. Developing the market in both cases required more capital (more cost) than the perceived value to the customer, and, therefore, they failed.

Entrepreneurs are forward-thinkers, but sometimes, timing is everything. As both Albert and Audible's Don Katz have learned, the market often needs to catch up with entrepreneurs. It is incredibly costly to develop a new market from scratch, even for the greatest, most creative entrepreneurs.

On the Lookout for New Opportunities

As mentioned in the previous chapter, by the time Raymond Baker joined Singer, sewing machines were a mature market. Raymond did himself and his family a great service by leaving this mature business environment, taking a risk, and moving into the mechanical testing equipment business that was quickly expanding in the mid-twentieth century. As the manufacturing base in the United States expanded, the needs for different equipment required to test manufacturing processes and end products also grew rapidly. Raymond hitched his wagon to this marketplace in which new innovation was built on new innovation. When the testing business started to mature, Raymond once again heard the call of a new market. As Dustin Hoffman learned in *The Graduate*, "plastics" was a quickly evolving market. Unlike Hoffman, however, Baker followed this path.

When I started with Gore, I worked in their sealants division. Sealants was one of Gore's oldest and most established products. I basically sold gaskets to chemical and industrial manufacturers that the company had been dealing with for several decades. Years before, Gore developed several solutions that changed the sealant marketplace, but by the time I was hired, most of the patents for those products had expired, and they were generally considered commodities. If you are an entrepreneur, commodity businesses offer little stimulation for your creative juices. The only difference between your product and the competition is price, which larger companies can keep low by using their economies of scale.

As soon as I realized that I was working in one of Gore's more mature (a.k.a., stagnant) business units, I kept my ears open for other markets within the company where innovation was needed and valued. After several months, an opportunity finally surfaced. It involved a new material called STA-PURE® tubing that Gore had developed for the biotech industry. While I knew nothing about biotech products, that put me on a level playing field with everyone else in the corporation. I had no official title regarding this new product (as mentioned, no one at Gore had traditional titles), but I served as the product manager for STA-PURE® tubing. The product was far from a salesperson's dream. True, it had an undeniable competitive advantage, but it was literally a hundred times more expensive than the alternative. Fortunately, there was an upside: learning to fight the battle of price versus value was critical to my understanding of the sales process. Anyone can learn to sell a product by saying: "I will sell you the exact same product for five percent less." It was my challenge to convince customers that they could actually lower their costs by spending a hundred times *more* than their original budget.

Focusing on Value

How did I accomplish that? Let's start with the basic concept of value in use. Value in use is the ability to understand what your customers' costs are prior to using your product and your skill to demonstrate how your product can change these costs (hopefully for the positive). Reaching an understanding of a value in use requires a salesperson to build a relationship that extends beyond the simple supplier-customer model; it requires both parties to understand each other's needs and capabilities. With STA-PURE® tubing, for example, we met with large biologics manufacturers, reviewed their manufacturing processes, and quantified the number of failures and cost per failure of the competitive product. It turned out that some customers averaged about three tubing failures a year, at a tallied annual cost of $250,000 per failure. Then we demonstrated that our tubing was unbreakable and explained that while buying our product would initially cause their tubing costs to rise from $1,000 to $100,000 per year, their tubing failure costs would decrease from $750,000 to zero. This created a value in use benefit of $651,000: ($750,000 + $1,000) – $100,000 = $651,000. This type of equation coupled with hard scientific data helped us to understand our customers' needs and focus on products that brought them true value.

Truly Listen

Of course, no matter how clever we entrepreneurs think we are, the best business ideas come directly from our customers. While I generally consider myself a decent ideas man, I have learned to become an excellent listener. So while we all want to talk about our great ideas, it's critical for entrepreneurs to stop for a moment and listen to what the market needs from them at this point in time. If you don't stop to hear it, the "Idea of the Year" may pass you by.

What you should know:

- *Make sure you can complete this sentence: "Our business brings value to society by __________."*
- *If at all possible, quantify your product's purpose and how it brings value to society. Hard numbers are very convincing.*

- *The greatest opportunities for entrepreneurs are in quickly evolving markets. Avoid mature markets. Listen to the changing needs of the marketplace.*
- *Focus on finding customers to whom you can provide a compelling value proposition.*
- *The best ideas typically come from customers—listen.*

Eight

The Art of Being Poor

As I mentioned before, I was so young and inexperienced when we started Mitos, I didn't realize that angels investors and venture capitalists even existed. In essence, I did not know that there were businesspeople who invest in start-up companies; I just assumed that if you wanted to create a company, you borrowed or saved the money yourself, and then plunged right in.

Saving Grace

After I graduated from college and was working at my first "real" full-time job at Gore, I chose to live at home with my parents for a while in order to save money. Eventually, I accumulated about $20,000. I know, the last thing most young people want to do after they graduate is return to the nest with mom and dad, but if you are determined to start your own business, it's important to save as much money as possible, and that includes spending rent money for an apartment. I meet many young entrepreneurs who yearn for all of the perks and rewards of owning their own business, but are unwilling to accept sacrifices along the way. Temporarily living with your parents—no matter how much you love them—or any type of alternative housing *is* a sacrifice, but if you are serious about saving some cash, you must find a way to live frugally. In the early stages of your venture, when you are the only person willing to fund your idea, that money will certainly come in handy and make it all worth it.

Necessity is the mother of invention, especially in the early years of your business when you are trying to survive without money. When I meet with the owners of early stage businesses, I can often tell instantly how they have been funded. For example, companies that have bootstrapped—that is, used their own money to start the company—typically are housed in modest offices with limited amenities. They also tend to be more team-oriented and less hierarchical. I think this is because bootstrappers usually have to scrape by together early in the development of their business. At Mitos, I was the lowest paid employee for the first two years and did not earn the company's highest salary until five years after we began.

But whether you pay for your company's launch yourself or have investors, most businesses must find some type of financing. It's the old "it takes money to make money" concept. The ideas proposed in this chapter are somewhat unorthodox and will not apply to every business, but they may have parallels for anyone interested in starting or looking to fund businesses and provide some outside-the-box options to financing.

Strap on Your Boots

Let's start out with this very basic premise: if you are a novice entrepreneur, you will initially have to bootstrap your business until you start making headway. With the exception of DreamIt Ventures (an early stage venture firm that I cofounded after the sales of Mitos) and some other very unique early stage funding sources, there are limited sources of funding if you are a young entrepreneur with an idea that's been scribbled on a napkin. So, unless you win the lottery or have rich, generous relatives who are eager to back you, you will probably have to initiate your business by bootstrapping. This doesn't mean you will not leave this path if the opportunity presents itself, but consider it your starting point. The more a business progresses (or reduces its risks), the easier it is to raise money. Unfortunately, I notice that most virgin entrepreneurs focus purely on raising funds to propel their business instead of concentrating on the development of their idea/product. But fundraising takes a tremendous amount of time. If a business uses its time and resources solely on fundraising, it may fail to move the business forward at an optimal pace. This creates a circular, catch-22 scenario that leads nowhere. Instead of taking the fundraising route, spend your time and resources establishing the value of your products or services to potential customers. Once you make headway proving the viability of your business, raising funds will prove easier and more time efficient.

When I left my job at Gore, all I had to start a company was an idea for a product, zero financial backing, and only a small amount of my own savings. My goal was to sell a customer on the idea and have them pay me to develop the product. My idea was a physical product. My goal as I developed this product was to protect the intellectual property the best that I could without any money. I hoped to do this by having someone pay for the product before it had actually been mass produced. I always felt that finding outside partners (and by "partners" I do not mean ownership partners, but businesspeople whom you respect and with whom you want to work) was a priority.

Here is a breakdown of how I did it:

Step 1: Suppliers. I consider it a blessing that I started my business in the middle of a recession. Why? Because lean times caused excess capacity, and suppliers were hungry for work. If I'd started in a boom time, it probably would have been more difficult to find someone willing to work with a twenty-four-year-old armed with nothing more than an idea and a computer-aided design (CAD) drawing. I sought out several suppliers, developed a long-term concept that benefited them and my fledgling company, and convinced them to make a prototype that I could present to customers.

But our goals and those of our suppliers had to closely align for the partnership to succeed. For example, a supplier who wants to sell ten million units of a product will not last with a customer who plans to purchase a thousand of the same product. Company values should also align. If a supplier believes in making the cheapest product possible and a customer values quality, it will probably lead to "divorce." The size of both the new company and the supplier also affects the balance of the relationship, especially if a small company purchases from a large company. Small companies are accustomed to resolving issues with a handful of employees, while bigger corporations need multiple meetings with a large group of people to accomplish the same result. With this difference in culture, the smaller company may eventually feel frustrated with the apparent inefficiency of a larger organization.

The world is not a zero-sum game. If you need mathematical proof of this, read the "The Origin of Wealth." As previously noted, in a zero-sum game, an economic pie is worth $10. When two parties interact, that pie's value remains at $10, which means if party A gets $7, party B only receives $3. But businesses can expand the $10 pie. For example, the right partnerships can create a valuable product or service for society and increase the value of a $10 pie to $15, leaving party A with an $8 slice and party B with a $7 slice, a win for both.

However, some people focus more on the slice that others receive rather than concentrating on the sizable portion they will take from the transaction. Negotiating and working with these types of people may prove difficult. Using the above example, if folks see the world as a zero-sum game, they'll assume that if party A accumulates $7, there will only be $3 remaining. Or they may not care that their take increased from $7 to $8 because they are too busy feeling jealous that party A increased their wealth from $3 to $7. With this type of personality, there is a deep self-centeredness and insecurity that makes them unwilling to commit to decisions that will advance others if, in their limited view, it will benefit the other party more than themselves. When you are looking for suppliers to partner with in the early years of your business, it is wise to avoid zero-sum game thinkers.

In Sync

One of the most productive partnerships in my life was with a man named Bob Elbich. Bob had already founded and sold a successful manufacturing business and was a second-time entrepreneur. Although Bob was thirty years my senior, we bonded instantly. I saw in Bob an excellent businessman, engineer, and person. Bob had just started his second business a few years earlier and was still in the process of growing it. Our mindsets were similar, we both valued quality above all else, and we each had a mission of creating a relatively low-volume product. Bob and I saw an opportunity to grow our businesses together. Bob knew that Mitos had limited funds, but I was able to convince him that our product would bring value to a customer base, and our company would undoubtedly succeed. After in-depth discussions, Bob and I developed a partnership whereby he accepted most of the financial commitments early on and was paid back in full once Mitos started to grow. Bob and I protected each other by jointly owning some of our Mitos patents, which provided him with the security to continue as our supplier in the long term. Yes, we had a contract, but more importantly, we had an understanding. With a lot of hard work, Bob and I eventually turned a $10 pie into $100. Beyond the rewards of the products and services of our partnership, Bob served as a mentor, a superb example of someone who had started a business from scratch and built it from the ground up. His guidance and experience was critical for me as I learned to navigate through the early years of Mitos, and I would not be in the position to write this book without his help and guidance.

> **Step 2: Protection.** In the early stages of Mitos, to protect our business ideas, we used different sources to manufacture various components of our product and then controlled the final assembly of the product so that no single supplier had a full picture. (Yes, this meant that my apartment was an assembly line some days, but as I mentioned before, in the beginning stages you do whatever it takes to make your dream a reality.)

It is a scary proposition, revealing all or part of your business idea to others. I wish I had a dollar for every person who told me about his or her a great idea, but was hesitant to share it with anyone for fear that it would be stolen. While this certainly is a valid concern, if you cling to this mentality, your "Next Great Idea" will stay with you—and only you—forever.

So how do you find the precise way to protect yourself while exploring ideas to grow your business? Here are a few guidelines:

Premise 1. The more people with whom you share your idea and the more feedback you receive, the more you can refine, improve, and expand your idea. DreamIt Ventures was developed under the premise of putting about forty intelligent entrepreneurs in the same office for three months to exchange ideas and help each other perfect their concepts. DreamIt works because each entrepreneur shares ideas with a diverse group of enthusiastic, innovative businesspeople and emerges with an idea that has been refined or sometimes changed completely because it has been reviewed, tested, tweaked, and challenged.

Of course, you do not want to be frivolous with your idea. Don't provide critical details when you are out at a dinner party! Never throw your idea out on the Internet. Proceed with caution. If your antenna goes up and you are concerned about sharing your idea with potential competitors or others, ask the parties to sign a non-disclosure agreement, which you can find online and print out. Use the "need to know" principle, meaning share only what others need to know in order to receive feedback from them.

If possible, file provisional patents. At Mitos, we filed the least expensive provisional patents possible to minimize costs. To many businesses, patents are critical, but expensive. One of the most cost-effective lessons I learned was to never give an attorney a blank piece of paper. There are several reasons for this: (1) legal work incurs many hours that can prove very expensive; and (2) giving a lawyer a base to work from ultimately leads to a more complete product to meet your specific needs. My Mitos team and I wrote the majority of our patents, so that our lawyer only had to cover the brief-yet-critical claims section that explained why our product was patentworthy. This collaboration was very economical for our young company and yielded excellent results.

Premise 2. While ideas are free and easy to create, executing a business idea is often expensive and difficult. Why do so few ideas turn into products and services? The answers are simple: (1) ideas are often not viable, which is why premise 1—sharing your idea and gathering feedback—is so important;

and (2) the difference between success and failure for a good idea is execution. You can't just talk the talk; you have to walk the walk. Much of this book is dedicated to allowing others to learn from execution, successes, and failures. The execution of an idea—transforming a dream from a sketch on a napkin into a business—requires more than just believing in a concept; it necessitates hard work, creative problem solving, and strategic thinking.

> **Step 3: Customers.** The main crux to finding customers is to offer a business, product, or service that brings value. At Mitos, our first product in the biotech field brought tremendous value to potential customers—it was a product that benefited their business—so they were willing to pay us up-front for it. Persuading a customer to pay for your product or service ahead of time will not be feasible for every new business, but you never know until you try. If customers are willing to spend money for a product/service that is still in the testing process, it's a good indication that it will bring value to their company (if it meets their expectation, of course) and your product is addressing a real need. The greatest validation of a viable product is a paying customer. And if customers are confident enough of your product's or service's quality to pay for it up front, that also reflects well on your company's reputation among potential investors.

When I was in the process of developing Mitos from an idea to a reality, I approached customers with a beta model in which I demonstrated the value of our product. I found an initial customer and then several more who were willing to try the product. It turns out that our first product stunk. After the customers tried it, they were asked if they would consider buying it, and they unequivocally said no. However, they also told us if we changed x, y, and z that they would pay for the alterations. This enabled us to form a strong partnership with our customers by listening to their needs and in essence making them part of our team. It also made it much easier to convince them to use our payment terms which were 50 percent at time of order and 50 percent net-30 (meaning payment was due 30 days after the product was delivered). This allowed us to use the money from orders to pay for the manufacturing of the products. We also used the customers' needs to drive our product development priorities. Eventually, these first customers became raving fans of our technology. From the start, they did more to market our product through word of mouth than we ever could have.

When you are building your new business, pursue as many customers and channels as your resources will allow. Most of the world's industries (especially in the United States) have various types of distribution channels. Building a sales force may prove expensive and time consuming, so consider building cost-effective, efficient channel partners instead. Channel partners are people in the marketplace with whom you partner for your mutual benefit. For example, instead of paying sales reps to exclusively market for Mitos, we paid manufacturers' representatives who sold other products to sell for us on commission. Yes, you may have to sacrifice some profit margin to motivate your channel partners, but more often than not, it will prove worthwhile.

Help, Please!

When searching for appropriate channel partners, I connected with a man named Dwight Long. Dwight's father, Don Long, founded Integra Companies during the 1973 recession. Before he started his own business, Don spent fifteen years helping to build another company. One day, the company owner's son took over the business. The son considered Don a threat to his authority, so he presented him with a pink slip and a $5,000 profit-sharing check. Don set out into an uncertain economic climate, but he decided to launch his own industrial supply business nevertheless. "It was scary but I really had few other options," Don recalls. With a wife, four young children, and two mortgages (one for a new home and another for their old home that had not yet sold), Don decided that it was time to take his life into his own hands and make his own destiny. And so, with the complete support of his wife and family, he bet it all, took his $5,000 profit share "parting gift," and formed a company that he felt could fill a need in the marketplace.

Like almost all entrepreneurs, Don's path was far from smooth. With no connections to wealthy investors, he took on a partner who added little to his business and whom he eventually had to buy out. After a few months in business, his biggest supplier cut him off. (Dwight Long still remembers the letter his dad received from the supplier. "It almost put my family on the street," Dwight recalls. "My mother had tears in her eyes as she used food stamps to buy groceries to feed our family of six," Dwight's younger brother Doug remembers.) Like most optimists, when a customer said he was going to place an order, Don took him on his word. He learned the hard way that an order is not an order until it is signed, sealed, and delivered in your hand. And these were just a few of the roadblocks Don encountered as an entrepreneur. As his business evolved, Don often went without receiving a paycheck, but he never missed the payroll for his employees. That built fierce dedication from his staff. To this day, Win Elliott and Gerry Mitchell, two of his original team from 1975, remain loyal members of the company.

Despite facing numerous obstacles over the years, Don built a solid business in the 1970s and 1980s. When the bottom fell out of manufacturing and customers started to close up shop and move overseas in the early 1990s, Don and his two sons, Doug and Dwight, decided to chart a new path. At the time, few businesspeople knew or understood the biotech industry, and the Long men were no different. However, they knew enough to recognize an industry with incredible growth that was actively supported by regional governments. That sounded much more desirable than the sagging industrial supply industry.

And so Don and his two sons changed Integra's course to meet the needs of the biotech industry and continued their push for the American Dream. By the time I met Dwight in 2000, Integra had grown into a regional powerhouse, controlling most of the consumables used by biotech companies throughout New England. Like his father, Dwight was never driven strictly by money, but by a commitment that he had learned from his father to bring value to his customers.

Dwight saw in me a younger version of his father. For him and his brother, the hardships that their family endured while their dad struggled to establish a thriving business instilled in them a feeling of pride in their accomplishments and a sense of responsibility to help others along the way.

Integra was our first channel partner and distributor. Signing on with such a prestigious and respected company provided Mitos and our products with instant credibility. This recognition was just a small part of how Dwight helped us and used his connections across the globe to link us and our products with distribution throughout the world. While Dwight viewed helping other entrepreneurs as payback for his family's success, he also saw the world as a non-zero-sum game; he knew that helping Mitos build market recognition would benefit Integra as well by making it easier to sell the product. Essentially, the reason why our fledgling company and Integra's established business meshed so well was because we shared similar values and our missions aligned. We had various relationships with other companies, but the Integra partnership ignited our organization and proved to be just the type of channel partner that our early stage business desperately needed.

Eventually, You Must Jump off the Cliff

One of the most frequent questions entrepreneurs ask me is: how do I get started? It's tough for them to conceive of initiating their own business because they are usually already working for someone else and need that secure income to survive. In addition, if they create any ideas or products, their employers will claim them as their own. As described in chapter 9, it is critical to analyze your business concept as much as possible before making an irreversible decision such as leaving your job. However, to be a successful entrepreneur, I believe that at some point you must jump ship from working for someone else to focusing on building your own business.

The timing of this shift will be different for everyone. When I went out on my own, it was scary, but I was twenty-four, had no mortgage, no wife, no children, no debt of any kind, and I could survive on less $1,000 a month. However, the person with whom I brainstormed the idea of Mitos and who considered leaving his job to help me found the company had a mortgage, a wife, and five children. In other words, because of his family obligations, he felt that he was simply unable to take a leap into the unknown. Timing, therefore, depends on your individual status. Regardless of your particular circumstances, prepare for this journey. Since my goals at Mitos were to develop product sales, I looked for means of supplementing my income that would also enhance my ability to sell our goods. Eventually, I became a manufacturer's rep, selling products to biotech end users and receiving a small commission. In addition to helping me pay the bills, the position enabled me to develop relationships with people within the industry. It also allowed me to start building our Mitos brand before we had manufactured actual products. In essence, this job provided exposure for Mitos and self-employment for me while I focused time and energy on building the business.

Without it You Will Starve

If "cash is king," then cash *flow* is its beating heart. Unfortunately, in the early incarnation of Mitos, we had no cash, but we used our customers' and suppliers' cash to grow our business. How? Many of our customers were Fortune 500 companies that were willing to negotiate payment terms. Early in our business, we gave a 2 percent discount to customers who would pay within 10 days of receiving our product. We also approached our suppliers and explained that, while business was quite brisk, we were an early start-up with limited cash. With this in mind, we negotiated thirty- to ninety-day payment terms after product delivery with many of our suppliers. These terms were accepted by our suppliers because we communicated openly, honestly, and followed through on our promise. If we had negotiated net-thirty terms after buying from our suppliers and then failed to pay until after ninety days, we may have lost them. In the early days, Mitos negotiated an average payment to suppliers of about seventy days. This meant we had to use every dollar we made from sales, minus a 2 percent discount, for 60 days. So if we reached a million dollars in annualized sales, we had an additional positive cash flow of $160,000 to use. Granted, this was expensive—a 2 percent discount is high for a struggling company. However, for us, it was the difference between making or not making payroll. With our growth rate of about 30 percent or more per quarter, this cash-flow model enabled us to increase our funds to the point that banks actually agreed to meet with us to discuss the possibility of a loan.

Yes, as I stated earlier, banks do not lend money to start-ups, even in the best of financial times. In 2001 when Mitos was born, most bank officials would kindly pat you on your back with a hearty "goodbye and good luck" if you had the gall to request a loan for a company with zero or negative assets. I was blissfully unaware of this fact when I took our Mitos business plan to almost a dozen banks in hopes of garnering a loan to jumpstart the company. After I realized that no bank was going to lend us money, I changed my tactic. I altered our business plan to reflect the supplier and net pay discounts to create cash flow and again met with several banks. I told them: "I know you are not going to lend me money now, but this is my business plan, and I am going to exceed the projections, so promise me that you will keep this paperwork, and I'll return a year from now to apply for a loan." Of the half-dozen bankers with whom I tried this approach, one banker, Bill Lang, kept my plan. I returned twelve months later with a year's worth of financial records that exceeded my original projection. Bill Lang had not read the plan, but he had not thrown it away either. He remembered me and was entertained by my optimistic approach. Once he reviewed Mitos' financial records from our first year in business, it was clear that we had not only accomplished our goals but, in fact, had exceeded them. Bill studied the numbers and then agreed to open a $50,000 line of credit for us. I wanted to jump for joy, right there in the bank, because at the time, the money was absolutely crucial to Mitos' growth and development.

If a business is successful early, selling equity is an extremely costly way to raise funds to aid in its growth. For example, if Mitos was valued at $500,000 when I received the $50,000 bank loan, I would have had to sell almost 10 percent of the company to raise the same amount of money. The bank charged me 7 percent interest, which may seem pricey, but the cost of selling equity would have eventually equaled a loss of several 100 percent when I sold the businesses (owning only 90% as opposed to 100%). So consider your options before you sell equity, and try a creative approach, even if bankers initially tell you to have a nice day and send you on your way.

What you should know:

- *If you want to start a business, save...save...save.*
- *Find the right partners who share your goals and values and see the world as a non-zero-sum game.*
- *First-time entrepreneurs almost always have to bootstrap their business; accept this and make it part of your plan.*
- *Find as many mentors and role models as possible.*
- *To perfect your "Great Business Ideas," share them with others, but do so judiciously.*
- *Determine a path forward that allows you to make a living and focus on your business.*
- *Manage your cash flow creatively.*
- *If you are successful, avoid selling equity because it is a very expensive means of raising money.*

Nine

Risk versus Reward

Starting a business is so daunting that many entrepreneurs literally do not know where to begin when they have an idea for a company or product. With a thousand thoughts rushing through their heads, entrepreneurs ask themselves questions such as should I start by: building a product model, conducting market research, seeking assistance from others, or writing a business plan? Arguably, any of these examples could serve as a jumping-off point for a new business. However, over the years, I have learned that a business in its embryonic stages is just a set of ideas. It is not yet a product or a service; it is simply an *assumption.* So with this mind, I believe that the early goal of a business—before the PowerPoint presentations are launched or the funding sources are solicited—is to prove or disprove these assumptions as quickly and cost-effectively as possible.

What's the Big Idea?

As we discussed in chapter 3, good entrepreneurs possess the courage to move ahead with a business plan even though they are not armed with complete information. While this tolerance is an admirable trait in an entrepreneur, be sure to balance it by acquiring as much information as possible as you proceed. Of course, total information will not be available, and you will be forced to make decisions with incomplete details; however, these situations should be minimized whenever possible. Why? Acting blind (without information) increases risk, and your goal as an entrepreneur is to reduce risk while maximizing reward.

Now, why is it so vital for entrepreneurs to address assumptions? Assumptions can make or break a business. Think of it this way: It is a given that every entrepreneur is bursting with ideas. But most entrepreneurs—me included—are lucky if one out of every ten ideas actually becomes a viable product or business. What makes that one-in-ten idea stand out from the others? I have discovered that the success or failure of transforming ideas into successful products or ventures usually boils down to the accuracy of a handful of assumptions that I call "core assumptions."

Core assumptions are the building blocks that inspire you and convince you that an idea can grow into a business. Accuracy of these core assumptions is what you'll need to prove to yourself—and your future team, customers, and investors—that your idea is viable.

But here is the tough part about core assumptions: in the planning stages of a business, these core assumptions are seldom accurate. In fact, I have found that, at best, they are typically only marginally correct. One of the key differences between successful entrepreneurs and those who continually fail is the ability to evolve their "Next Big Idea" as more information becomes available. Successful entrepreneurs seek out new information and attempt to continually prove the accuracy of their past information. Early in the development phase, it is almost impossible to know everything that is required to build a business, such as meeting customers' needs. If you *expect* your idea to change instead of clinging stubbornly to your original concept/business plan/marketing strategy, you'll save yourself much angst and disappointment.

Getting to the Core of the Matter

To keep it simple, remember this: if your core assumptions are wrong, the business is wrong. This doesn't mean that a business will necessarily fail if the core assumptions are off.

Why? Because if you recognize that one of the elements of a core assumption is incorrect, you can adjust your idea early in your business planning.

From a numeric standpoint, core assumptions are often the numbers in a spreadsheet that if you change even minutely—for instance, one-tenth of one percent—after five years, that small percentage can affect your profitability by 1,000 percent. Core assumptions, therefore, drive your product or business, your partnerships, your customers, and often, your exit strategy. They can literally mean the difference between success and failure, so even if one of your core assumptions is wrong, it will change *everything*.

In essence, core assumptions reflect the structure—the key elements—of a business. If any of these elements fail to meet with initial projections or expectations and are not identified, they will eventually prove to be the root cause of a business's failure. It's best to figure out how something can fail *before* it fails so that you can build it better from the start. As an entrepreneur, you will create a stronger business if you can test, prove, and adapt your business idea. This will ensure that you address the potential failures of your business from the get-go, before the business fails.

How do you determine your core assumptions? While every business is unique, core assumptions can usually be placed into the large categories that represent most businesses, including:

- Demand (huge problem)
- Product differentiation and positioning
- Customer need / value proposition
- Product-development capabilities and timeline
- Market size
- Price the market will bear
- Selling cycle
- Execution capability
- Competitive response
- Financial requirements

Let's look at a scenario to clarify this thesis.

Suppose the five core assumptions of your business are as follows:

(1) Monthly Web traffic will increase 10%.

(2) Sign 7.5% of all new traffic to free three-month subscriptions.

(3) After three months of free subscriptions, 20% of existing traffic will continue to pay the $9 monthly fee due to the fact that, for these customers, the product reduces their costs by $10 per month.

(4) Expect 1% of subscriptions to be cancelled annually (i.e., churn).

(5) Infrastructure base costs will be $2,000,000, with up to 50,000 users.

Now, if all of these assumptions are correct, the business will return a profit of $1.35 million in year five. However, suppose all of your assumptions are accurate, except one. Let's say that assumption number three is incorrect, and only 10 percent of people continue on with the paid service, which results in a half million dollar loss in year five. In other words, the difference between a 20 percent and a 10 percent conversion rate assumption could signify the difference between spending time chatting with Donny Deutsch about your success or living at the ratty motel down the street because you lost your business, your home, and your dreams. Realizing that this assumption is incorrect allows you to ask the bigger question: why is our product not bringing the value that we believe it should? It could be that you are not reaching the customers you thought you would; it might be that the customer does not understand the value proposition; or it simply may be that the product really does not bring the value that you thought it would. However, the earlier you identify this inaccuracy, the better chance you have of making adjustments to the shortcomings.

This example illustrates that you need confidence in your core assumptions, *and* you must prove that they are correct. This ultimately reduces the risk of starting a business, which will catch the attention of those who are interested in investing in your new venture.

A Look at My First Mistake with Core Assumptions ...

A strong yet simple example of a core-assumption mistake involves my college-era business mentioned in chapter 4. My friend David Suarez and I decided to sell carpets to incoming freshman. Our core assumptions (even though we didn't call them that at the time) were that:

(1) About a quarter of the freshman moving into the dorms would need carpets for their rooms.

(2) If we were strategically located at five destinations throughout the campus dorms, we could approach the freshman and sell to those who needed new carpets.

(3) We would purchase 250 carpets in bulk for $20 each.

(4) We could sell the carpets for $40 each.

So how did we fare? Not great. Our failure did not lie in that we did not identify the core assumptions; it was that we simply did not know enough to prove or disprove any of them beforehand.

It turned out that all but one of our assumptions was correct. Unfortunately, when a Penn State security guard kicked us off campus, we were miserably wrong on assumption number two (execution capability), our selling locations. Because we were no longer nestled right next to the dorms, we lost our competitive advantage over the local carpet stores. Looking back, if we were more experienced, we would have proven these assumptions to be true *before* spending everything we had—and then some—to start the business. David and I could have played the core assumption "what if?" game by challenging each other with different scenarios, including this key question: what if security tells us to "beat it," and we have to vacate the premises? We could have adjusted by either obtaining permits from the university or securing other locations that would have provided us a leg up against the competition.

While this is a relatively uncomplicated example of unchallenged core assumptions, it is *exactly* the type of trap into which I see many first-time entrepreneurs fall into. So while it is great to be passionate about an idea, don't let your excitement blind you to the fact that there may be some flaws in your plan.

Live and Learn

By the time I started Mitos, I had learned plenty from my numerous core-assumption mistakes along the entrepreneurial path. So as the idea for Mitos came to fruition, my team and I recognized the importance of first identifying our core assumptions and then building a business plan embedded with an excellent financial model. Spreadsheet number one of this financial model included our core assumptions as:

- Our perceived need in the marketplace.
- The financial numbers to prove this need.
- How our core assumptions of need and finances translated into the success or failure of the business.

Like all businesses, our core assumptions were very specific to our company. Here are two of our core assumptions, one that was correct and one that was not:

(1) Our first assumption (product differentiation) was that Mitos' valve technology had a significant advantage over the existing valve in the marketplace. We assumed that this advantage enabled us to charge about $600 per valve, compared to the existing competitive product that was priced at $400. With our first few potential customers, we were able to test this $600 assumption by showing the value that our product brought to them and the money it would eventually save them, even though it was priced 50 percent higher than their current model (value vs. cost). We listened to the customers' feedback, which was universally positive, and soon concluded that our product was fairly priced at $600, and customers would not object to the cost. We were then able to build our business plan with this $600

price and hard data to prove the accuracy of our assumption.

(2) Another assumption (customer need/value proposition assumption) that we had during the initial phases of Mitos was that some potential customers would be willing to convert their exiting valves over to our technology at a very modest rate of 1 percent of the market per year. For the sake of illustration, let's say that our estimate of the existing value market was $250 million. We assumed that it would prove difficult to convert existing valves to our product (which is why we estimated it at only 1% of the market), but unfortunately, our assumptions were optimistic. Why? Virtually no businesses in the market wanted to convert their existing technology to our product because the move would have required that they submit the change to the FDA. We could have charged $1 per valve, and the value proposition to the customer would still not exist. For us at Mitos, the difference between our 1 percent assumption and zero was $2.5 million in revenue, a figure which obviously changed our entire business plan. We identified our inaccurate core assumption early by tracking our sales by location versus our financial model. By catching it early on, we were able to make adjustments to our plan and focus exclusively on approaching companies that were building new biotech plants. If we had continued down the path based on our original assumption and built a sales force and infrastructure banking on an additional $2.5 million in revenue, we would have faced a difficult hurdle, to say the least. Perhaps more important, proving that this assumption was incorrect allowed us to focus our limited resources as a company in the areas in which we had the best chance of success. Had we continued to focus on existing biotech sites, we would have diluted our efforts at new sites, which would have resulted in zero sales at existing sites and reduced sales at new sites.

Obviously, for the purpose of illustration, both of these original assumptions have been oversimplified, but they demonstrate that we tackled these assumptions and developed ways to test them as early and cost-effectively as possible.

One of the greatest challenges that entrepreneurs face is the fact that they will have to execute a plan with very few resources. Proving and disproving core assumptions will help you to focus these resources in a manner that will help optimize your returns. Why spend time trying to sell your product to a market that doesn't recognize its value when you could be selling it to a more appropriate market?

Test, Test, and Continue to Test

When you are starting to map out your business, analyzing your core assumptions is akin to testing a hypothesis and trying to prove or disprove it. If your assumption is "the world needs product Z," find ways to quantify if this is true, and test your assumption. Challenge others to disprove your assumption. If your assumption is proven to be incorrect, ask bluntly: why? If you do not like the answers, ask yourself what you can change about the business that will create a more favorable outcome to the assumption.

This process of refining core assumptions allows entrepreneurs to fill the need in any given marketplace. Challenge your assumption, even if your funds are limited. As Steve Barsh states on his blog BarshBits.com, if you cannot afford to test a hypothesis, find a proxy or substitute experiment/market study. When we launched the Mitos valve technology, we had no sales history. However, we could point to other technologies that had been successful in the industry and demonstrate similarities between those products and ours, as well as their business types and ours. From this point, we could show the sales cycles and market-adaption rates of the similar products and correlate them to our valve. This provided a logical starting point to build our financial model.

Be sure to track the data of your assumptions, because results will change as the business climate evolves or as competitors notice your success. As entrepreneurs become consumed in their business, they may not recognize changes in the market. I often find that entrepreneurs do not anticipate a competitive response. As mentioned before, with the Internet and other technological advances, the world moves faster than ever, and if a business starts to garner market share or alter a market in any way, a competitive response will quickly appear. Monitoring core assumptions will likely help you to recognize the competition and how it affects your business early on. The beauty of this thought process is that it will also force you and the entire business to focus on what is important and what will likely have the greatest affect on your business.

As an angel investor, I am privy to hundreds of business plans a year and dig deeply into about four of them every month. I am amazed at how often business plans fail in what I believe is the most critical element of the document: identifying and monitoring core assumptions. Accuracy of these assumptions represents the risk of the business, and without them, no investor or entrepreneur can fully understand the risks—or opportunities—associated with the project.

It Doesn't Always Take a Million Dollars

With core assumptions in mind, let me tell you about a young entrepreneur named Bryn Davis.

Bryn is the type of entrepreneur who cannot be ignored. A dedicated, persistent fellow, once he discovered that I could become a potential investor, he simply had to tell me all about his idea. Bryn had developed a concept for a new type of food business that focused on healthy fare while maintaining the desirable attributes of fast food, including convenience and speed. He had also devised some other unique means of increasing revenue by utilizing this fast-food model to provide healthy lunches to schools.

Bryn was charismatic and energetic, and once I spoke with him on the phone, I could feel the passion in his voice. I sensed that he was not just a dreamer, but had already taken sacrificial steps to make his business idea a reality. What intrigued me most about Bryn was that he had identified his core assumptions. Although he did not have them written down, I knew by the manner in which he explained his business idea and its incumbent risks that the core assumptions were clearly in his head.

While I was impressed with his enthusiasm, when I first met with Bryn in person, I was also taken aback by his statement that, like so many entrepreneurs, he needed a large amount of money—$500,000—to start his company and was totally focused on raising those funds. Although I wanted to help Bryn, I had to be honest and tell him that it was not the ideal economic climate (fall, 2008) to raise a half-million dollars for an unproven company with loads of risks. That said, I did not want to discourage him, so we began a quick brainstorming session. For fifteen minutes, we more formally identified his core assumptions and, just as important, created scenarios to prove or disprove his core assumptions. It was a critical fifteen minutes for Bryn's company, and it didn't cost him a dime. The ideas from this brainstorming session inspired Bryn to return home and start small, gradually building his healthy food business out of his house and proving the soundness of his core assumptions. Bryn began using his intellectual capital instead of financial capital.

At the earliest stages of a business, it is critical to creatively find ways to manage the financial risk of starting a new company. At Mitos, once we identified a need in the marketplace that we felt was sufficient enough to address, we explored the idea by developing an inexpensive prototype of our product and asking potential customers to test it and provide feedback. Early on in the business, I created some designs of our product and attempted to obtain customer feedback, and while this was often helpful, I eventually realized that nothing can replace an item that a customer can touch and feel. Likewise, Bryn is marketing products from his home kitchen to demonstrate a market need. Neither of these ideas cost much, but both provide a tremendous validation of the value of the product and, in turn, minimize the risk of the business for the owner and for potential investors.

Whether Bryn will succeed or not is still unknown, but I am confident that when he approaches me and other investors again in a year with hard data and revenue to back up his assumptions, I will not only be more willing to listen, but more likely to financially support his venture. Since he will have fewer assumptions, it will decrease his risk and increase the value of his company.

To Each His or Her Own

Business plans are strongly emphasized in business schools. In my opinion, however, detailed business plans are a waste of time if you have not first sketched an outline of a business and identified the core assumptions that are needed to turn the idea into a viable company. A business plan maps out the future state of a business, supported by proven core assumptions; without confidence in these assumptions, there is no confidence in your future business.

While there are entire volumes of books dedicated to business-plan writing, most fail to recognize that different businesses require different approaches. For example, I have seen a Web-based company obtain funding to build a business based on a ten-slide presentation. (By the way, this success is uncommon and almost never happens for first-time entrepreneurs.) I have also seen a hundred-plus page business plan with a fifteen-year time horizon used to support an early stage biotech company. Each plan was totally different from the other, and each was appropriate for the individual business. Yet the common trait of these and all good business plans is the thought process that demonstrates how the current state will turn into the future state by demonstrating the soundness of the assumptions and proving their accuracy or, at a minimum, providing ways to prove their accuracy.

Well-known entrepreneur John Osher, who has developed hundreds of consumer products, compiled a brilliant list of everything he did wrong and saw other entrepreneurs do wrong to create "17 Mistakes Start-Ups Make." I strongly believe that fourteen of these seventeen pitfalls can be avoided by correctly identifying and testing core assumptions. (The remaining three pitfalls will be addressed in subsequent chapters.)

Entrepreneurs, Take a Deep Breath and Focus

Like exuberant young children, many entrepreneurs want to delve right in and begin building their business. However, this is one area where entrepreneurs should demonstrate a more cautious viewpoint. Core assumptions are the basis of any business, whether it is a $100 million business unit in a Standard

& Poor's 500 company or a fledgling start-up being hammered out on a kitchen table. Core assumptions drive a business, and if you build a business on the shaky foundation of incorrect assumptions—even if the rest of your materials are solid—your company may collapse. Stay strong by valiantly proving and disproving the soundness of your core assumptions.

What you should know:

- *Once you have identified an idea, the next step is to identify the core assumptions that are required to turn your great idea into a viable business.*
- *Proving the accuracy of your core assumption will reduce the risks while at the same time demonstrate the rewards. Reduced risk equates to increased value.*
- *Find capitally efficient ways to test the assumptions. If the assumptions are off, be flexible, adjust, and try again.*
- *Focus on spending human capital prior to worrying about financial capital.*
- *Use your core assumptions as a guide to focus your resources on the areas in your business that will have the greatest impact on your success.*
- *Build a business plan* after *you are confident in your core assumptions.*

Ten

The Team

Should you acquire an equity partner?

Every early stage entrepreneur asks this question at one time or another, and it deserves some thought because your decision will impact your business *and* your life.

Let's start by reviewing the benefits of going it alone. It's a short list, because I believe there are only two real advantages to forgoing partners. First, as a solitary leader, you can make decisions, act quickly, and avoid ownership struggles that often engulf companies. In addition, as the sole owner, you can benefit from the company's rewards during the life of the business and—potentially—when it is sold. In short, the advantages of sole ownership are power over decision making and control of all profits.

On the other hand, the advantages of equity partners are enormous. Properly structured partnerships provide you with emotional and collaborative support and bring financially committed individuals into a business. Perhaps more important, the best partners create a cohesive team that increase the knowledge base of a business and therefore increase its likelihood of success. While having partners can prevent you from ultimate decision making, collaborative thinking usually results in wiser choices, which lead to a bigger pie. Even though this pie must be shared, its greater size means more for everyone. So eat up because, as previously mentioned, the world is not a zero-sum game.

Lonely at the Top

At Mitos, I ended up going it alone, but not because I chose to. As noted before, the person with whom I had discussed the business in its earliest stages was simply unable to make the leap from an established job to a start-up. When he decided not to join me, I had to follow a solitary path. After the intense grief of September 11, I would have done almost anything to lean on a partner for support. Not only was it a difficult time personally because one of my best friends perished in the Twin Towers, but business basically shut down for a period, and customers were canceling orders as we slipped deeper into a recession. To add to my angst, John Blaha, a key employee who worked for us part-time, decided to move closer to his children and resigned his position. With more than thirty years of experience in manufacturing, John's level-headedness complemented my overexuberance; he was my voice of reason, my sounding board. While his departure was necessary for himself and for Mitos (we would not have been able to pay his salary when business stalled after 9/11), it created a lonely world for me. It proved to me that partners bring critical emotional and collaborative support, and when you are nurturing a business in its early stages, you need all of the help and camaraderie you can grab.

Go, Team!

When you are building a team for your company, look for diverse skill sets. This is never more important than in an equity partnership.

For starters, diverse skills enhance your overall ability to make decisions by providing a larger knowledge base from which to work. This larger knowledge base reduces risk. Most successful partnerships that I have seen have one person who is very strong in sales and marketing and one who is very strong in either technology or operations.

Some may argue that you can hire partners, meaning that you bring on employees who in essence act as partners without ownership. If all else was equal and I had to bet on:

- Company A, with a single owner who was strong in sales and marketing and intended to hire operations and technology people or;
- Company B, with three owners, one who was strong in sales and marketing, one in operations and one in technology,

I would bet on team B every day of the week and twice on Sundays. Why? Bottom line: owners have different motivations than employees. Due to their financial and emotional commitment to the business, owners are willing to work more hours and sweat through challenges instead of throwing in the towel when times are difficult.

Although I am preaching about the advantage of partnerships, I do so with a word of caution because many such collaborations fail (which may subsequently cause the business to fail). I believe that most partnerships collapse due to poor communication and flimsy up-front planning. Entrepreneurs get so swept up in the process of creating a business that they do not take time to discuss and plan for "what if" scenarios with their partners.

Proceed with Caution

If you choose to add equity partners to your business, do so cautiously. There is no rule that a partner has to become a full partner on day one. If you have a business up and running and want to acquire partners, find ways to create a trial period for all involved parties. Allow them to prove that they can bring value to your business and earn their equity. If you offer a person half of your business without any commitments, it may be impossible or at least very expensive to reverse that decision.

Many entrepreneurs quickly collaborate with partners, only to find out that the partner is unable or unwilling to pull his or her weight. Don Long is a perfect example of this. When Don began Integra Companies, he invested $5,000 of his own money, but his partner didn't contribute a dime. When Integra faced difficult times, it was apparent from his partner's actions—or lack thereof—that it was Don's money on the line. It took Don ten years and some unfortunate mishaps to finally buy out the dead weight partner. In hindsight, I think Don would agree that he should have granted equity to his "partner" *only* if certain milestones were met. For example, if Integra needed a million dollars in revenue to support the company's infrastructure, Don could have created a simple agreement stating that his partner's equity would be granted as long as that million-dollar goal was met within three years. This would have provided his partner with a powerful incentive while simultaneously protecting Don from the burden of a partner who was unable to pull his own weight.

While there are typically two individuals in a business partnership, I feel that it is usually more efficient and safer for one of the parties to have a controlling interest. Of course, most entrepreneurs, by nature, want to be the party in control. However, in most partnerships, there is a natural leader who emerges. If you are that person, be sure to exercise your leadership skills early on in the planning stages by obtaining 51 percent of the business.

If you choose to start a fifty-fifty partnership, however, I strongly urge you to find an outside investor to buy a small percent of the company. Although this individual may own only one or two percent of the business, he or she will prove indispensable when difficult decisions must be made, and you and your partner need someone to serve as a tiebreaker.

Another option for two-party partnerships is what I term the "nuclear clause." The nuclear clause is a provision in an operating agreement that allows either party to approach the other party and make an offer to buy the company for a set price. The other party then has the option to either accept the offer or purchase the company from the other party for that same price. Obviously, this is a very risky proposition for the party making the original offer because it places them on an irreversible path in which they have no control. Like a nuclear standoff, if both parties have the option to launch a weapon that may well lead to their demise, they will consider it a last choice and try to work through their differences instead.

First Things First

While leadership certainly sets the stage for culture, individual team members are the ones who act out the play.

Due to the unique skills needed in the early stages of a business, the first few people a company hires are the most critical *and* the most difficult to find.

At Mitos, I was involved in hiring every employee, and I considered it one of my most important jobs. When interviewing prospective employees, I was cognizant of two important points:

(1) I needed an understanding of my own weaknesses and strengths in order to hire someone to offset or complement those weaknesses or strengths, respectively;

(2) I needed employees with the mind-sets that fit well into our small-company atmosphere.

Although it's human nature to surround yourself with like-minded individuals, there is a reason why animals that interbreed too closely pay the price in the long run. Likewise, diversity is critical to the evolution of ideas. Biology 101 is: differentiate, select, and amplify. In that same vein, the evolution of an idea works by creating new concepts, selecting what works, and then amplifying them. The marketplace continually accomplishes this as new products and services are created. Most individuals have limited capacity to think through a number of concepts; however, a team of individuals can much more efficiently try new ideas and, just like the natural mechanism of the marketplace, choose what will work best.

Building Blocks

Building a team is more of an art than a science. This process should be broken down into two distinct categories: skill set and mind-set. A strong team needs a diverse skill set. At minimum, a team needs a person who is strong at sales and another person who is strong in operations. Without both of these, ideas and businesses fail. More broadly, sales encompass the ability to take new ideas, develop and present their value proposition to a potential customer, and close the deal. Without this skill set, a company will not get off the ground. More broadly, an operations person is the individual who can turn an idea into a tangible product or service in an efficient manner. Without this skill set, a company may lift off the ground but will quickly fall back to earth. In addition, many companies also need a team member who is strong in product or service development. Although distribution or commodity-based businesses may not need this individual, businesses based in technology development will absolutely require this key person.

Skill Set	Person
Sales & Marketing	
Operations	
Research & Development	

While it is easier to visualize and map out skill sets on paper, it is no less critical to build a team that has a diverse mind-set. A mind-set is the natural ability to work and make decisions comfortably. Here are some examples: some people are strong on details and short-term goals, while others excel at working on the big picture and long-term horizons. Some individuals are consistently calm and levelheaded, while others are bouncing off the walls when times are good, but despondent and immobilized when times are bad. Some individuals are inherently creative and out-of-the-box thinkers, while others bring an element of practicality to the process.

Mind-set	Person	Mind-set	Person
Big Picture & Long-term Horizons		Details and Short-term Horizons	
Passionate and Energetic		Calm & Levelheaded	
Creative		Rigid	

It is critical to make sure that all of the boxes above are filled and relatively balanced. If you build a team of ten individuals and nine of them are "big picture" people with only one "details person," you are destined for trouble. (Plus, the detail-oriented employee will become so overworked that he or she will probably quit.)

Chapter 3 outlines the traits that characterize many entrepreneurs. It is critical for start-ups to build teams of people with strong entrepreneurial traits and skills. The most critical trait for your first employees is ambiguity tolerance. Early in the development of a business, the future is murky, and a person must be comfortable working in an unpredictable environment. It is also important for team members to feel comfortable taking on many duties.

Michael Ryan came to Mitos as an engineering manager after working for five years at Lutron, a relatively large company that manufactured dimmers. After several weeks at Mitos, Michael realized that the trash in his office was piling up. Late one evening, he discreetly asked a coworker if she knew who was responsible for taking out the trash. After a good chuckle, the coworker told Michael that he (Michael) was. Michael didn't mind emptying his own trash, but this story illustrates a difference in mind-set from those who work in larger companies, where employees have focused responsibilities, to small companies, where everyone wears numerous hats, including those of janitor. At Mitos, we looked for individuals who embraced the concept that no job was too big or too small. Building a team is not a process that starts when you need an employee and stops when you find them; instead, it is an ongoing ebb and flow that the best companies in the world recognize as a true art form.

When I started building a team at Mitos, I knew what I was searching for, so I pulled out my Rolodex and looked for people who fit those needs. When the name Charles Meadows first appeared, I instantly took a trip down memory lane. I first met Charles in sixth grade, and he remained a close friend throughout high school, but I had not seen him in several years. From a mind-set standpoint, I knew that he was the ying to my yang. While I was a big-picture guy, Charles was the type who could build a tedious spreadsheet from the bottom up. While I was passionate, he was a calm person who never soared too high nor sunk too low. While my general mind-set was all about practicality, he was a creative thinker. The challenge was that he was a sales and marketing person, like me, but I felt that Charles' personality could adapt to any environment. He had a unique temperament that allowed him to fit into a company of any size. In addition, I knew Charles from the time we were children, and most important, I knew that he was a good, honest, and trustworthy person who would help build the Mitos culture in a manner with which I was comfortable. Although having two strong salespeople and no operations person on our Mitos team worked for a period of time, it certainly made life a lot more difficult for us in the early years, and our company struggled to succeed until a strong operations person was in place.

A Day's Pay

When I first approached him, Charles had a good job and was doing very well. At the time, there was no way that I could match his existing salary. However, Charles saw the unique opportunity that Mitos offered and thought it would be fun working with his old pal, so he took a cut in pay in return for a commission schedule that would payoff greatly if we were successful.

Compensation is one of the most difficult issues for small-company owners to tackle. Big companies have established pay structures that everyone knows and accepts. Corporate managers claim that they certainly *want* to give their employees more money, but they are restricted by pay guidelines. But in a small company, every employee knows that the company owner is the only one who can allocate pay raises. This situation causes tremendous stress because, whether it is right or wrong, as a society we generally equate salary with one's worth.

I recommend three tactics to address this issue:

(1) Do not hire people who view pay as the sole driver in job selection. People must be paid fair wages, but if money is their primary driver, they will probably leave the company as soon as they receive a higher offer elsewhere. Individuals who are solely motivated by money often internally miss the concept of constructive self-interest, which can make them ineffective team players who do little to promote a culture rooted in purpose.

(2) When hiring employees, be sure that they feel they are being fairly compensated for their job. I ended every

interview with a potential employee with this sentence: "Knowing our benefits package, which includes full medical, 100 percent company match of up to 7 percent for our 401k, and profit sharing, what would it take for you to feel fairly compensated at Mitos?" If their number was in line with what we could afford to pay for the job and what we felt the market would bear, that was great. Likewise, if someone's salary expectations are not in sync with yours, evaluate the job and determine if the person's needs are out of whack with the position's responsibility or your figures are out of touch with the current job market. If your company is offering a competitive wage, don't force a square peg into a round hole.

(3) In order to avoid discrepancies, outline pay increases on an annual schedule, and communicate this to all employees. Clarify that the only other salary increase will be for added job responsibilities. This will avoid mid-year calls for pay increases that can distract managers and employees.

All in the Family

What about including family members in your business partnership? I have participated in several entrepreneurship panels over the years, and that is one of the most common questions I hear. This is a very personal topic that individuals must decide for themselves. I have very talented people in my family, but for me, the risk of losing a relationship far outweighs the potential reward of having a dedicated member on my company's team. I know a grandfather who has never even met his granddaughter because he and his daughter had a falling out over the business they started together, so that has taught me to separate business and family.

On the other hand, the Long brothers, who were mentioned in chapter 8, are an ideal example of family partnerships. They work independently, with Doug handling the operations, with final say on all operational matters, and Dwight overseeing sales, with final say on any sales-related decisions. The brothers work respectfully if any issues happen to overlap these two categories. Like a good marriage, they do not keep score. No one brother claims that he works harder or that he has a more difficult job; they respect each other for the skills that they bring to the business and inherently trust the other's efforts or motives.

In any relationship, there will inevitably be someone who works more hours or is paid more in a certain market, but a partnership requires a bond to work together as equals, no matter what occurs. This should be true not only of family partnerships, but all business partnerships as well.

Good Advice

By definition, beginning entrepreneurs lack experience. One of the most effective means of overcoming this hurdle is to build a board of advisors. To do so, many entrepreneurs compile a list of powerful names to attach to their business. While these successful people can help shed light on the workings and requirements of a new company, keep in mind that those people typically have little or no time to spend helping a start-up company. Like building a strong team, compiling a strong group of advisors requires diversity. Yes, Bill Gates will undoubtedly add credibility to your venture, so he does bring value, but this industry giant does not have the time to mentor you on a weekly basis. For this reason, be sure to not only include big names on your advisory board, but also respected individuals who have the time and the dedication to help you succeed. I also recommend offering your advisors some performance-based equity in your company to provide motivation and encourage personal involvement with your new business. I believe that one of the greatest values DreamIt Ventures (more about DreamIt in chapter 12) brings to entrepreneurs is pairing them with mentors who have equity in DreamIt and therefore have a vested interest in helping the company to grow.

What you should know:

- *Bringing in partners increases knowledge base and thus reduces risk.*

- *Equity partners bring value, but ensure that the structure is well planned and protects all parties.*
- *Early hires are the most critical. Find people who are comfortable with the following mentality: "No job is too big or too small."*
- *Building a team is constant work that requires balancing both skill set and mind-set.*

Eleven

The Exit

If you ask Dave Willis about the exit strategy for his company, his reply is simple and concise: "in a wooden box."

Dave precisely recalls when he began his journey as an entrepreneur: December 22, 1964, at 9:15 a.m., the exact moment when he was fired. Dave spent his twenties working for and building up a small manufacturing business in the quickly expanding filled Teflon molding compound and reinforced thermoplastics market. A young executive named J. Tracy O'Rourke had come to power within the company. A politician who had the ear of the owner, Tracy considered Dave and a handful of other employees as threats to his ambitions and lobbied for their dismissal.

As a suddenly unemployed twenty-eight-year-old father of four children, Dave decided to do what he knew best: sell filled Teflon compounds. He borrowed a small amount of money from his father (another entrepreneur) and formed Whitford Chemical, a manufacturing operation that added fillers to Teflon. Dave used loans from banks and customers to finance the business. He established a relationship with one bank that allowed him to borrow money against accounts receivable. He still remembers shipping orders to a customer, walking to the bank, and receiving a check from the bank for the value of that shipment. He also learned how to prioritize suppliers' payments. Dave realized that big companies would not cut off a customer, so he negotiated material consignment and extended-payment terms with them.

After just two years, Whitford Chemical grew bigger than the company that had fired Dave. Several years later, in 1969, he noticed that the market was becoming very crowded and decided to sell his fillers business to focus on a new technology that the company had developed. Dave felt that the product—a nonstick coating with endless applications—showed great promise in a wide-open field.

Bigger and Better

And he was right. He changed the name of his business to Whitford Corporation, and the company soon exploded into the field and evolved into a global supplier of fluoropolymer coatings for everything from plastic to rubber to metal. If you have a nonstick pan for cooking, you probably use a Whitford product.

Although Whitford became a huge success, its history is dotted with many close calls. Dave vividly remembers the company almost going completely under in 1978 when a supplier covertly changed the formulation of the product they supplied to Whitford. Suddenly, Whitford was selling a product that did not meet specifications. While they diagnosed the problem quickly and made good on their customers' orders, they lost 40 percent of their business in four months and were forced to lay off almost half of their employees.

As so often is true with entrepreneurs, Dave's business troubles affected his personal life and family. For example, financial troubles forced his oldest daughter to put off college until after the company recovered. Uncomfortable with the financial stress, Dave's partner of ten years took a job with another company and left Dave to rebuild Whitford on his own.

But rebuild he did, and today Whitford is forecasting 2009 revenues of $150 million with operations in every major industrialized country in the world. 72 years old, Dave arrives at the newly constructed headquarters at about 6:00 a.m. with the same enthusiasm he had when he founded the company over forty years ago. He continues to have close contact with customers and drives new and innovative products that meet their varied needs. While he could certainly sell the company and ride off into the sunset, Dave is an entrepreneur who loves what he does, so why would he leave?

I met Dave when I had just started Mitos and was working out of my apartment. Dave graciously offered me office space at Whitford, and I jumped on the opportunity. Dave never charged me a dime for rent or requested anything else in return; instead, like so many other successful entrepreneurs, he simply wanted to give back in the same way that others helped him along the way.

Exit, Stage Left

In the fall of 2006, I approached Stephen Goodman of the Morgan Lewis law firm. Steve is often referred to as the godfather of the Philadelphia start-up scene. You name a successful start-up story in Philadelphia in the last thirty years, and Steve has been involved with them. I was honored that Steve agreed to meet with me. In preparation for our meeting, I wrote and rewrote Mitos' five-year business plan and finally sent it to Steve.

At our first meeting, I waited in the conference room on the top floor of the Morgan Lewis building in Philadelphia. I was expecting a formal type of lawyer to appear in a perfectly tailored power suit, meet with me for five minutes, recommend that his firm represent Mitos for all of our needs, and instantly hand me off to an associate.

But I was wrong. When I first met Steve, I was surprised that he was dressed in a casual yet stylish sweater and sport coat. It was instantly apparent that Steve had carefully and thoughtfully read our business plan cover to cover. I hoped that Steve could help devise a plan to move the business forward. Mitos was expanding at an astonishing clip, and growth was accelerating. This amazing success was tying up all of our capital—and then some. We had a new building under construction, and with the changing marketplace, I wanted to grow the business more quickly. I knew that we needed outside capital to meet the cash flow required for the construction and our growth plans. I hoped that Steve could help us raise money from private equity and venture capital firms. After we shook hands, Steve and I spent a full hour exploring every possible option for Mitos. In that sixty-minute period, he taught me more about business funding and mergers and acquisitions than I ever knew. I realized immediately that Steve was not a stereotypical lawyer, but a thoughtful, creative entrepreneur. By nurturing Mitos through our growing pains, he knew he could eventually bring great value to himself, his firm, and his clients.

With Steve's guidance, we branched out into a new world of private equity and venture capital. We hired a small but powerful investment bank called Fairmount Partners. Fairmount's Neal McCarthy and his team built a powerful case for Mitos' value with the goal of raising money by selling a small stake in the business. With this successful team, we received several offers to buy a large portion of the company, but it was clear that accepting any of them would essentially force me to work for someone else and hold only a minority stake of equity in Mitos. I also started to understand that the venture/private equity firms had what was termed a "fund cycle," which meant that their goal was to deploy all of their cash (buy companies) in a few years and then harvest the returns (sell the companies they had purchased) in five to seven years. This was driven by the fact that the venture/private equity firms receive money from outside investors who want it returned with gains as soon as possible. If I chose to sell the majority of my company to one of these funds, I would probably be forced to sell the rest of the business in five to seven years. So if I decided to take money from outside investors, I would either have to parcel off my company in pieces in a set amount of time or sell it all at once.

Check It Out

Over the years, Mitos had been approached by various players in the biotech industry who wanted to acquire the business. With Whitford's Dave Willis as a role model, I was leery of meeting with any of these suitors because I planned to continue building my business into the foreseeable future. However, after receiving several intriguing offers from financial buyers, I gave Fairmount the go-ahead to contact all interested parties and investigate the possibility of selling the business in its entirety. Eventually, after a bidding war between several Standard & Poor's 500 companies, Mitos was sold. The market conditions were perfect, and we were able to select a suitor that we felt would continue to grow the business. While we did not accept the highest offer, we selected one that we believed would benefit all stakeholders, including employees, customers, distributors, and me. Letting go of Mitos happened by chance; prior to the sale, I had no interest in selling my "baby" and was growing the company with a long-term view.

In my mind, hunkering down for the long haul is the only way to build a business. But in today's "get-rich-quick" society, I see many entrepreneurs focusing on an exit strategy (that is, the point at which they sell the business or form an IPO) when they first create their business plan. The root of this is probably the MBA mentality that focuses on raising money from outside investors as the main means of building a business.

Outside investors also mean outside agendas, which often run counter to the founder's objectives. For entrepreneurs and investors, this focus on exit strategy is a mistake. Here's why:

(1) Many of the variables required for an exit are outside of one's control.

(2) Businesses built with this mentality (one in which the founders and investors aim to exit the business in a short period of time) miss out on building the most critical elements of a company: culture and purpose.

All the Stars Aligned

To exit—or at least exit at the best value—market conditions must be perfect. This macro issue is relatively random, and building a business model around something that is completely out of your control is dangerous. There are also specific industry issues that must align, and while they can be forecast to some extent, they are by no means always accurate. There are times when smaller, more nimble businesses will bring the most value and other times when consolidation is necessary to bring value to the industry. Every business is different, but every business should act like a child trying to strive for self- sufficiency. If the opportunity presents itself to sell, merge, or IPO, and the conditions are right, make the move at that time, but do not focus your resources on exiting from the get-go.

It is very difficult to build a culture of trust when the underlying idea behind the business is to sell it in a specific period of time. In certain markets and businesses, especially ones in which many or all of the employees are shareholders, this may work, but even in these instances, such thinking creates shortsightedness. One of the primary reasons that public companies fail is that they are so focused on immediate results that they become unwilling or unable to make short-term sacrifices for the long-term benefit of stakeholders. Companies that are building their business on an exit plan are likely to succumb to the same shortcomings.

At Mitos, we focused on growing the business long term. Therefore, if we did not sell when we did, the company would have continued to grow. Had we cut the business back in a desire to make it appear more attractive to suitors and then not sold it, we would have been in a weaker position long term.

About a year after selling Mitos, I began looking at businesses that were for sale, but I soon realized that companies were cutting costs in an effort to appear healthier. When the mergers and acquisitions market collapsed in 2008, however, there were no buyers, and these companies were left managing businesses from a weaker position with slower growth. Companies that optimize their value for stakeholders, even if they are up for sale, do themselves a favor in the long run. In addition, if the need arises, it is always easier to sell a growing, profitable business with a strong culture and an established team.

I am not suggesting that businesses should ignore exit opportunities; on the contrary, I think they should constantly review all options, including exits. However, companies focusing on long-term-value create the most exit options. Dave's exit plan of a wooden box is one way to focus on long-term value creation.

What you should know:

- *Taking on outside investors brings agendas that often differ from those of the founders.*

- *Understand your potential exit strategies, but focus on developing long-term value. A profitable, growing business is easier to sell.*
- *Exit only when the timing is right for you and your team.*

Twelve

Oh, the Webs We Weave

Soon after I started Mitos, I was out on a second date with a nice young lady. Immediately after dinner, I received an emergency call from one of our biggest potential customers. They had an entire batch of product on hold because they could not get the perfusion pump that I had sold them to function properly. So at 10 p.m., my date and I rushed over to the manufacturing site—threw on sterile protective gowns—and went in to a clean room where I tried to fix a pressurized pump without compromising the product. After several hours, I was successful, and my customer was grateful, but my date was not. Although I lost the girl that night, I had gained a customer for life.

I do not blame my date for her displeasure. I can see how someone would have been irritated if her date dragged her out to a strange manufacturing building while she sat there and watched him try to diagnose and fix a malfunctioning pump. But the entrepreneur's life is different than those who work nine-to-five. There is no "work day," and there is also no vacation because you are always at the beck and call of your employees, customers, and suppliers. The operations at Mitos ran five days a week, twenty-four hours a day. It was not uncommon for me to receive a phone call at 2 a.m. that necessitated a middle-of-the-night dash to the plant to fix a problem. Even when I was not physically at work, like all entrepreneurs, my mind was constantly at work. Starting a business requires a commitment not only from the entrepreneur, but from everyone in his or her life.

The Right Surroundings

The summer I turned sixteen, I met Nicole. On the outside, she was awkward and shy, but as I got to know her better, she was fun and passionate. We enjoyed our summer romance, but went our separate ways when fall arrived, mainly because we went to different schools.

I dated other girls after that, but it was my best friend Nicole who I eventually married. I am not sure if it was her accepting personality or simply the fact that she and I grew up together, but she respected and understood me for better or worse. She was more risk averse than I was, but had enough trust in me to overcome the uncertainty that I constantly brought to our lives in my crazy entrepreneurial ventures.

Nicole and I did not get married until Mitos was well on its way to becoming a successful company. This was probably best for both of us. While I am sure we would have been fine, I spent so much time building the business that it would not have been fun to be married to me in the early years of Mitos.

Even after we were married, I continued to work long hours, but Nicole understood that I didn't labor for money, but for the love of my work. She recognized my passion and my need to give 100 percent to my projects. Simply put, without her ongoing support, my life and my work probably would have been vastly different.

The best decision I made in life was to marry Nicole.

Family is the heart of any support system. For entrepreneurs, there is nothing more critical than marrying someone who is supportive and understands and openly accepts the risks of starting and running a business. All the entrepreneurs profiled in this book recalls a time when their entrepreneurial adventures took time away from their family, and all of them also credit their family's support as one of the most—if not *the* most—important factor in their success.

It is also important for entrepreneurs to expand this support system as early as possible. Building a business from scratch is different from almost any other experience in the world because the founder makes the final decision in its success or failure. We often forget how unique a situation this is. There is no boss to complain about because "the buck stops here." It can prove daunting and isolating. I made the mistake of not building a support system outside of my family in the early years of my business, which led to some very lonely decisions and unsettling times for me.

To this day, I still vividly remember "John Doe," the first person that I ever had to lay off. John was actually hired at I-4, a company I started with five other people after Mitos was founded. The other five principals of the company were spread out geographically, and, for a variety of reasons, we wanted the business positioned in Pennsylvania. Due to these circumstances, I was left to run the business on a day-to-day basis. Two of the other original I-4 founders and I performed the search and the hiring process for the company's general manager position. This was in 2002, when the job market was very weak, so we literally received hundreds of resumes for our job posting. After reviewing all the resumes and interviewing a handful of people, we settled on John. Although John had been unemployed for some time, we were impressed with his eagerness to return to work. During his twenty-five-year career, John had worked almost exclusively at larger companies. In hindsight, this should have been a red flag—not that individuals can't shift from big companies to small companies, but we should have dug deeper to determine if he could handle the transition. The general manager position was our first hire at I-4, and the role required an individual who could act independently with almost no oversight and little direction. After he was hired, it quickly became apparent that John could not handle the autonomy of the job. Although he was excellent at executing his duties when someone told him exactly what to do, the position called for an individual who could make decisions on his or her own. After providing ample opportunity for John to prove himself, we determined that the arrangement was not working out and decided to let him go. Because I was geographically the closest owner, I had to break the news to him.

John had lived a difficult life. With a strong background in industrial manufacturing and distribution, John had witnessed the mid-Atlantic industrial base disappear before his very eyes. He was in his fifties, but as a longtime smoker, he appeared much older. As I sat down with John, I realized that he was the same age as my father. I am sure that I stuttered and my voice cracked as I explained to John that the relationship was not really working out. He became emotional at the news and tears formed in his eyes. We talked for a while, and it was apparent that he was embarrassed to tell his family that he was once again unemployed. Although the day I had to let John go occurred many years ago, it lives in my heart like it was yesterday.

John's failure was mine. I had placed him in a position that was outside of his experience and mind-set. He suffered emotionally because of me, and I swore that I would never repeat that mistake with an employee. Since that day, although I have laid off workers because of poor performance, I never hired anyone without first making sure that I truly understood the company's needs and the prospective employee's skill set and mind-set. One of the most important tasks of an entrepreneur is selecting a strong team; I was involved in the hiring process of every single employee at Mitos until the day I sold the company.

At the time, while my family was supportive and understanding through difficult decisions and experiences like the one just mentioned, I would have done anything to talk with other entrepreneurs who were also starting a business and experiencing similar challenges and complex decisions.

Support, Please

Blake Jennelle graduated from Harvard in 2004 with a dual degree in social studies and mathematics. Blake made his money the old-fashioned way: online poker. As a mathematics major with a strong understanding of the Web, he was able to develop mathematical models into innovative software that provided him an edge over his online poker opponents. As is always true, markets evolve, and as others began to employ similar technology, Blake's competitive edge began to dissipate. Fortunately, Blake saw the writing on the wall and started to look for other ventures.

In the summer of 2007, Blake founded Anthills. Like most entrepreneurial ventures, Blake's business started when he identified a need in the marketplace. As a freelance Web developer, Blake saw a gap in the market. While the Web provided several solutions for freelancers, Blake believed there was a special need for high-end free-lance businesspeople. With his idea in hand, Blake set out to raise money to turn his concept into a product. He quickly learned that, as a first-time entrepreneur, raising money was very difficult. As he went from networking event to networking event, he also began to feel as if he was the only first-time entrepreneur trying to start a business. Eventually, when he connected with several other entrepreneurs, it was clear that they also felt alone in the world of launching a business. After coming across a dozen or so entrepreneurs, Blake decided to send out an informal e-mail to see if they wanted to get together and share war stories.

Eight people met at the Ten Stone Bar in Philadelphia in the fall of 2007. As Blake puts it, "It was as if a burden had been lifted off their shoulders when they realized that each of them was experiencing many of the same issues. They all began asking questions such as: 'Who do you talk to about hiring people? Who knows what law firms are the best for early stage businesses? What do you do if you have to fire someone?'" These are questions that all entrepreneurs have to answer at some point, but there is no how-to book or Web site that can effectively provide answers to complex and individualized circumstances.

Effectively answering these types of questions requires a close-knit social network based on trust and mutual respect. Like all good ideas, Blake's network quickly took on a life of its own, and suddenly, the scattered pockets of entrepreneurs throughout the region had a hub. That hub was later called Philly StartUp Leaders (PSL). It is a powerful network whose members have the ability to find others who can easily relate to their visions, ideas, and anxieties. As the PSL manifesto reads: "We thrive because we understand that, above all else, start-up entrepreneurs need each other."

Unfortunately, I did not find or build a network like PSL when I started Mitos. A support group would have been good for my emotional well-being, and had I been able to bounce ideas off of other entrepreneurs, I may have avoided some costly pitfalls. I commend Blake and the rest of those who built PSL for their work, and I encourage others to form similar networks in other geographical areas.

While PSL has flourished, Blake's original business, Anthillz, has since been closed down. Blake speaks with pride about the failure of Anthillz because it was an educational experience for him and because others can learn from his failure. Looking back, Blake feels that he focused too much on the development of what he terms "cool technology" instead of infiltrating the market with his product and pounding the pavement for customers. As he has subsequently learned, "Once you have customers, you can allow them to drive what the market needs. It may not be cool and sexy, but it will meet their needs." Since closing Anthillz, Blake has joined an incredibly successful start-up, TicketLeap, an online site for small events. I suspect that the team at TicketLeap finds Blake's experience at Anthillz more valuable than his degree from Harvard.

I am privileged to know Blake personally. I suspect that he will probably start another business from scratch some day because, like all successful entrepreneurs, Blake views Anthillz's failure as part of his deliberate practice, a building block for future ventures.

The Intermediate Steps of Success

At age twenty-five, when Mark Baiada (see chapter 6) had a meeting with himself and determined that he was falling behind his goal of getting where he wanted to be in life, he didn't just sulk and complain about that. Instead, he laid out specific goals and objectives on both a personal and professional level to achieve his goal. He did not just say, "I want to go out and start a business," he also added, "and here are the steps that I need to take in order to ensure the best chances of success." He built a list of priorities and allocated a set amount of time to each of those priorities. It did not happen overnight, but within two years, Mark was running his own business.

There is much written about building business plans, yet I find it shocking that there is scant literature regarding the concept of building a personal plan. While a personal plan brings value to everyone, it is especially critical for entrepreneurs, whose personal and business lives often blur together. Some people may have a personal agenda in their heads, but putting it on paper enables them to more effectively execute their plan and build the intermediate steps needed to achieve their long-term goals.

Getting to the top of a mountain is much less daunting once you are halfway there. By achieving smaller annual goals, an individual also creates a positive feedback loop. This feedback loop reinforces the process of deliberate practice, which in turn leads to success in the person's chosen field.

Here is the format for an annual plan. (I didn't create this format, and because I am uncertain who did, I apologize for not crediting him or her.) It is simple, concise, and it constantly helps me to prioritize my main resource: time.

(Insert year_______)BUSINESS AND PERSONAL PLAN

(Insert year______) BUSINESS ACCOMPLISHMENTS	(Insert year_____) BUSINESS DISAPPOINTMENTS
1. 2. 3. 4.	1. 2. 3. 4.

(Insert year______) PERSONAL ACCOMPLISHMENTS	(Insert year_____) PERSONAL DISAPPOINTMENTS
1. 2. 3. 4.	1. 2. 3. 4.

(Insert year_______) BUSINESS GOALS AND BJECTIVES

GOAL	MEASUREMENT
1. 2. 3. 4. 5.	

(Insert year_______) PERSONAL GOALS AND OBJECTIVES

GOAL	MEASUREMENT
1. 2. 3. 4. 5.	

(Insert year_______)BUSINESS AND PERSONAL PLAN

What will be my single greatest business and single greatest personal challenges in (insert year__________)?

What are the important changes/initiatives I must implement to ensure that I can make my (insert year ______) goals? And when must they be accomplished?

What was my single biggest business disappointment in (insert year_______)? What specifically am I going to do differently to avoid having a repeat of this disappointment in (insert year________)?

What was my single biggest personal disappointment in (insert year______)? What specifically am I going to do differently to avoid having a repeat of this disappointment in (insert year________)?

What you should know:

- *Find the right person with whom to share your life, someone who understands you and shares your values.*
- *Building a business requires commitment not only from the entrepreneur, but also from his or her family.*
- *Find or build support networks with other aspiring entrepreneurs.*
- *Building a personal plan and a business plan allows an entrepreneur to lay out the intermediate steps needed to achieve long-term goals.*

Thirteen

The Value of Time

A few years after graduation, in the summer of 2001, I was enjoying time with friends on the deck of a café in State College, Pennsylvania. My crowd had scattered in many different directions after graduation, and our careers were as diverse as our geographies, so some of us met for a mini-reunion at Penn State. I had started Mitos just six months earlier, and, as I surveyed the scene around me, it was gradually becoming apparent that I was beginning to embrace different values than my friends. At that point, I had spent most of my savings launching Mitos and was very cautious about my spending, which was in stark contrast to many of my old friends, who seemed to have no qualms about throwing money around. I tried to not judge them, but every time someone bought a round of shots for the whole gang, I couldn't help but think what I could do with that $200: pay for a week's worth of work-related gas and parking; cover several days salary for the customer service person whom I just had hired; or write a check for this quarter's health insurance.

Time = Money

That day at the café, it hit me that my value system had begun to shift. At that point in my life, I knew that I was short of two things: time and money. It took several years for me to understand that time and money are closely correlated.

Why? When you are poor, money has a very different meaning than when you are well off. When I was starting my company, money represented food and shelter to me. To many of my friends whose incomes far exceeded their basic needs, however, money was a means of obtaining entertainment and luxuries. When one individual looks at a $10 bill and sees food, and another sees a night at the movies, their values differ greatly, and it may prove difficult for the two parties to relate.

But money was not the only subject that I viewed differently than my contemporaries. While most of them had good jobs with a set schedule and fixed compensation, I worked long, unpredictable hours and had a totally variable income. I realized that it was going to take a good deal of my time to grow the business, and thus, to me, time *was* money. And just as important, money was time. I realized that neither could be wasted, and both had to be treated with respect.

Ever since then, I consider time to be the most precious, irreplaceable commodity in life.

Managing Your Time and Your Money

Ideally we spend our time on that which is most important to us. We balance the time between pursuing short-term and long-term goals in order to utilize our time in the manner that suits us best.

Although this book does not focus on personal finances, and because time and money are interchangeable, it is important for entrepreneurs to learn how to properly manage both money and time.

I do not worship money—far from it. However, I do worship spending time with my wife, reading to my daughter, learning, and pursuing my own interests. Most people I know also value quality time; I am attracted to and want to be surrounded by those who recognize the precious nature of time.

Yet I see many folks who live well above their means and then spend most of their time working to pay for their lifestyle. Because money is time, the debt they accumulate causes them to work more, which takes away hours they could have spent pursuing interests they enjoy. There is good debt and bad debt, but it is important to recognize that debt creates indentured servitude. I frequently hear people say how much they hate their job, but they stay with it mainly because they need the money to pay for possessions that have brought them little or no joy. These same people would probably be happier going to a job that they enjoyed, even if it paid less, than they are with all of the accoutrements that they bought with their current earnings. How much satisfaction can a mansion bring someone if they are never home to enjoy it and too busy working at a career that they positively detest? I am constantly approached by aspiring entrepreneurs who are extremely interested in starting a business, but hesitate to do so because they are already saddled with a huge debt that they are struggling to pay. Debt or lack of money reduces their options. If you focus on the accumulation of material goods, it can detract from entrepreneurial goals or other ambitions. Understanding your values and prioritizing your self-worth and satisfaction may help steer you in the right direction.

An "Up Close and Personal" Example

My parents were a team, and both of them worked to make our family unit strong. My father had a very stressful and demanding job, while my mother concentrated on an equally stressful and demanding job: raising our family and later, after we were in school, resuming her teaching career. Although I did not realize it at the time, my parents lived below their means. No, we didn't wear patches on our clothes, but my parents didn't worry about "keeping up with the Joneses" and were careful to live well but simply.

Here's an example. In the late 1990s, when my father was a successful executive at DuPont, he threw a party for his staff at our house. My parents always put my brothers and me to work at these types of affairs, so I was in charge of organizing parking for the party. I'll never forget the parade of high-end cars that arrived at our house that day. They were driven by people who reported to my father, so in theory they made less money than he did, yet while they owned Mercedes or BMWs, my father drove a 1977 Mazda RX7 that had rust holes in the passenger-side floorboard. (It was not without its amenities—after all, it had an eight-track player.) Several years earlier, my father decided that his wheels needed a new paint job. After receiving several quotes, which he felt were "ridiculous," dad decided to rent some equipment and paint the car himself. A nice paint job looks smooth as glass, but his work was as bumpy as sand paper. While I shuddered at the results, he looked at it, the finished product, with pride. In his mind, he had saved hundreds of dollars to add to his children's college fund.

As a child, I was none too thrilled with my father's bargain-basement tendencies, but today I understand how his thriftiness was purposeful and sensible. He and my mom worked hard, and we lived in a nice house in a nice neighborhood, but they did so without drowning in debt. By making sound choices and saving well, my parents were able to retire in their mid-fifties. Today, they pursue their own interests or passions and are almost like carefree children again, enjoying tennis several days a week and playing pickup softball games. They travel, exploring the world and seeing friends, and help to raise their grandchildren. For them, the money they saved for thirty years has translated into precious time, and it enables them to do what they want in life. Of course, they may choose to return to work at some point, but that will totally be their choice. What a wonderful position to be in after a lifetime of working and raising a family.

As you can see with my parents' example, everyone's priorities are different regarding time and money. I am fortunate to feel passionate about work, so the time I spend working is a pleasure. Most entrepreneurs feel the same way, excited to wake up every morning to get started on the latest project. But even with passion, remember to prioritize what you want in life and make wise choices so that you can spend your time as you wish. For example, saving an extra two percent a year in your 401k plan in your mid-twenties translates into the ability to retire three years earlier. Is saving an extra two percent a year worth three years of life in which you have complete control of your time?

The Time Value of Time

With apologies to all of my past teachers, building a business from scratch was the most educational experience of my life, and that would be true even if the company had failed. For more than six years, I was challenged, and my knowledge base grew daily. I struggle to recall a day when I did not learn something new about people, business, the marketplace, or myself.

Moving forward from this experience, I am in a position to convert my time into money at a far greater rate than when I was twenty-three and starting my company. This, in turn, means that I can work less to create the same amount of money, and, conversely, I have more time to spend on the things I choose to prioritize, whether it is my family, charities, or helping others to achieve their dream of building a business. Although I worked very hard to achieve these options, I still cherish and truly appreciate having them.

Most people know the time value of money, which states that a dollar now is worth more than a dollar in the future because of the compounding advantage of interest. But if time and money are interchangeable, what about the time value of time? This means that time today is worth more than time tomorrow because of the compounding advantage of, in this case, knowledge. If individuals use their time today to acquire knowledge, they can ensure having more time in the future.

$$(\text{Present Time})^{(\text{Knowledge})} = \text{Money} = \text{Future Time.}$$

Most of us inherently understand this equation, but may act as if time is limitless and do little to adjust for it. Because of the importance of both time and knowledge, there are two main advantages to starting a business when you are young instead of waiting until you are older and more secure:

1) If you are successful at an early age, you will have the money to do what you want with your time for a longer period of time.

2) Whether you succeed or fail, the knowledge you acquire through the journey allows you to translate your time into money at the greatest rate.

The Unacceptable Waste of Time

This type of freedom appeals to everyone, not just entrepreneurs. The greater your knowledge base, the greater your ability to utilize time, based on your own priorities. Like money, time compounds over time, so the earlier you gain knowledge, the better.

Most people understand the value of time intuitively; it's why people who work for companies that waste their time are so frustrated and unhappy. If I am at a company and spend two hours a day in meetings where I bring no value to others or learn anything new, about 25 percent of my work day is wasted and can never be replaced. I believe that individuals who find themselves in such a state are much happier when they break free of their mental and emotional rut, and find an alternative to survive and thrive.

There are people who will argue that they cannot leave their job because they need the money; however, if their time is being wasted, two issues are likely to occur:

1) If the company has a culture that leads to a great deal of wasted time (money), it will probably fold or, at a minimum, start to decline, and your job will be in jeopardy.

2) The company is diminishing your future ability to convert time into money by not optimizing your learning or growth. This ultimately will reduce your future earnings at other endeavors.

There is an entire body of work focusing on why people flourish in smaller companies, but I think that time is a root cause. Few large companies have been able to develop effective cultures/management systems that utilize their employees' time successfully. That's why starting a company or joining an entrepreneurial company is the perfect venue to enable you to respect your own time and money, and to ensure that others do the same.

What you should know:

- *Time and money are interchangeable; respect both.*
- *Understand your own values, and prioritize your time and money accordingly.*
- *If someone wastes your time, move on.*

Fourteen

The Power of Small

The story of David versus Goliath is one of our most revered tales. In America, this is deeply rooted in our Judeo/Christian belief system and in our historical tendency to root for the underdog. Our history is filled with examples of little guys who have persevered to achieve success when bigger, more established institutions have failed. As a society, we are an industrial and commercial Goliath; however, to assume that size is the key to success is to make a mistake as big as Goliath's when he approached David.

America is successful as a society not because we are a commercial and industrial Goliath; we are successful because we actually function as thousands of smaller, focused units—an army of "Davids." Over the past century, the U.S. economy has been the engine for wealth creation on a scale never before seen. The combination of our democratic political system coupled with a free-market economic system has empowered individuals to use their creativity and energy to achieve wealth for themselves while concurrently creating wealth and opportunity for others. This has been accomplished by ensuring that self-interest is aligned with societal or institutional interests, a concept I refer to as constructive self-interest.

Constructive Self-Interest

As the father of modern economics, Adam Smith's belief that the pursuit of self-interest benefits the world is correct yet incomplete. The pursuit of self-interest requires an understanding that society's interests and the individual's interest are closely related and not mutually exclusive. If one pursues self-interest at the peril of the rest of society, he or she may benefit in the short term, but society will be hurt in the process. Because individuals and their family live in society, their long-term self-interest will diminish.

For instance, Bernie Madoff stole tens of billions of dollars over decades in pursuit of his self-interest with complete disregard for society. While he benefited in the short term, he left many people void of trust—and of their life savings. His family and their heirs will be forced to exist in a world that he has left in his wake—a world with less trust, which will lead to reduced efficiency, which will result in a lower standard of living. Madoff may have read Adam Smith's words and taken them at face value, but he will have the rest of his life in prison to reflect on how his blind pursuit of self-interest at the expense of decimating thousands of people around the world led to his own self-destruction.

On the other hand, pursuits that benefit society as a whole also benefit the individual. For example, teachers spend tireless decades educating our youth. These individuals could make more money in another career, but by contributing positively to the world around them, they find purpose and bring great value to society, which, in turn, helps to create a greater standard of living for themselves and the rest of us. In its truest sense, *constructive self-interest* requires that the creation of something of value to the individual also contributes something of value to society.

I am Just a Little Guy

In the fall of 2006, the biotech supply base was being infiltrated by some of the largest companies in the world. GE, ThermoFisher, and Millipore were all making enormous acquisitions. I looked at these Goliaths entering the marketplace, along with consolidation in Mitos' customer base, and believed that we needed to get bigger faster. We had a compound annual growth rate of more than 50 percent over the five previous years, yet at the time I did not think that this was fast enough. Our cash flow and asset position would not allow us to grow more quickly, so I set out to raise capital.

Looking back, my concerns were logical but unfounded. In theory, large public companies have an enormous competitive advantage over small private businesses. They have virtually unlimited capital and huge resources. Utilizing their economies of scale and allocating their resources to areas with the best returns, big companies should be able to crush their smaller competitors.

But despite these advantages, data published by the U.S. Census Bureau clearly indicates that the bulk of new jobs are generated by firms with less than twenty employees. Net new jobs are the total number of new jobs created by firm start-ups and expansions (gross job creation) minus the total number of jobs destroyed by firm closures and contractions (gross job destruction). From 1990 to 2003, small firms (fewer than 20 employees) accounted for 79.5 percent of new net jobs, despite employing fewer than 18.4 percent of all workers in 2003. Mid-size firms (20 to 499 employees) accounted for 13.2 percent of the net new jobs, while large firms (500 or more employees) accounted for 7.3 percent. Not only are small businesses generating jobs at an amazing rate, they are a significant source of innovation and patent activity. Small businesses develop more patents per employee than larger businesses. Furthermore, small firms' patents tend to be more significant than those of large firms, outperforming them in a number of key metrics, including growth, citation impact, patent originality, and patent generality. These metrics have been used for decades to measure the innovation of firms, labs, and agencies. The metrics have been validated and shown to correlate with increases in sales, profits, stock prices, inventor awards, and other positive outcomes. This suggests that, in general, patents of small firms are likely to be more technologically significant than those of large firms.[11] This fact

[11] Breitzman and Hicks, "An Analysis of Small Business Patents by Industry and Firm Size," November 2008.

is even more remarkable when research and development (R&D) budgets are taken into account. Small high-tech businesses generate five times more patents per R&D dollar than large businesses.[12]

So why are small organizations creating so much more value than large organizations?

Short-Term View

The issue today is that many large companies are institutionally owned, meaning that no individual owns enough of the company to have a true vested interest in the long-term performance of the organization. This floating-ownership structure creates an environment whereby decisions are often based on short-term needs and what is best for the leadership of the organization.

What drives these short-term decisions? The need to report to Wall Street and concern about daily stock prices are two major factors. Remember, if no one really owns a significant stake in the company, then it is easy for anyone and everyone to exit the company by selling stock. Because a majority of leadership's compensation results from stock performance, top management acts in their own self-interest, which means doing what appeals to market analysts today.

Merrill Lynch is a particularly galling example of this. Late in 2008, Merrill Lynch was failing. The company was out of cash and requested a bailout from the federal government to continue operating. The government complied, and Merrill-Lynch received $10 billion of taxpayer money, which was supposed to be used to cover loan losses and shore up their balance sheet. However, Merrill Lynch's CEO used $3.6 billion of the designated funds to pay bonuses to top management. He and three other corporate officers received a total of over $100 million in bonuses, and 750 corporate executives received bonuses of over $1 million each. All of these executives enjoyed these outrageous sums, despite the failure of the company for which they were responsible. While the bonuses were technically legal, they were clearly not in the interest of the shareholders, and they were a violation of the taxpayers' trust.

---

[12] Small Business Technology Council, "Why Are High-tech Small Businesses so Important to the United States?," March 2008.

To test the premise that ownership aligned with a long-term view improves corporate results, just look at a study performed by third parties. With the help of Chicago executive-search firm Spencer Stuart, *BusinessWeek* identified the family companies in the current Standard & Poor's 500 and tracked their performance over the past decade. By and large, family companies were defined as those in which the founders or their families maintain a presence in senior management, on the board, or as significant shareholders. (In a few of the companies, the "founders" actually acquired the companies and substantially remade them.) For the family companies, the annual shareholder returns averaged 15.6 percent, compared with 11.2 percent for nonfamily companies. Return on assets averaged 5.4 percent per year for the family group versus 4.1 percent for nonfamily companies. And the family outfits trumped the others on annual revenue growth, 23.4 percent to 10.8 percent, and income growth, 21.1 percent to 12.6 percent.[13]

In this study, family ownership equates to a significant portion of the ownership focused on long-term growth (because they own enough of the company, they cannot easily sell it) that is aligned with the family's interests as shareholders. It is evident from the results of the study that this alignment makes a dramatic difference in company performance.

The Constructive Self-Interest of the EcoSystem

You may have noticed that few if any of the above issues arise in small or private companies. The owners of these companies have plenty of incentive to keep the interests of employees, customers, and suppliers aligned with their own; there is no vast reservoir of someone else's wealth to tap into for their own enrichment without successful value creation.

A successful company focuses on all of its stakeholders, as this is essential to value creation. Shareholders' interests are best served by ensuring that customers, employees, and suppliers are engaged, and their interests are served by acting in a manner that is aligned with the company's interests. These interests are tightly linked. I assure you that shareholder returns

---

[13] Small Business Technology Council, "Why Are High-tech Small Businesses so Important to the United States?," March 2008.

will be subpar if customers are not serviced properly, and I am positive that customers will not be serviced properly if employees are disengaged, demoralized, and disempowered. It is also likely that a company that does not treat suppliers well will in turn receive poor service, and thus, poorly service their own customers.

In Mitos' conference room, we had a saying framed on the wall: "Mitos is judged by the quality of life of its people, customers and suppliers." Employees who are not engaged in a business will not perform at their optimum level. However, employees who are engaged and, most importantly, are stakeholders in the company possess a dedication to the business that cannot be matched. Not only is employee retention greater at these companies, but customer retention is better because they recognize value in a partnership with people who are dedicated to the success of the entire ecosystem.

Customers ... Customers ... Customers

It is obvious that a company without customers will not survive, yet I am always amazed at how many companies build their operating structures without the customer as the focus. Building a culture around customer-as-key-stakeholder forces a business to build its operating structure with a focus on providing value to said customer. It also provides a culture that builds partnerships with customers, which is much more productive than traditional buy-and-sell relationships. At Mitos, customers drove our product development, and it was natural for our customers to participate in this process. By treating our customers as an extension of our business, as part of the same ecosystem, we were able to instill within them confidence that we would treat them fairly and share the rewards of our successful product development.

The same held true for Mitos' suppliers, who we treated as extensions of our business. We negotiated contracts that were true win-wins, which allowed our suppliers to build value through our growth and value creation. Suppliers are often as integral to a business as the employees themselves, yet I have seen more than one company treat their suppliers as second-class citizens. This sometimes results in lower prices and better profitability in the short run, but leads to a weak and disloyal supplier in the long run. In the same way that a company faces trouble if it has weak or disloyal employees, it will encounter difficulties when working with weak or disloyal suppliers.

Any party that touches a business is part of its ecosystem. While there are some diverging interests (most notably, competitors) in any ecosystem, for the most part, customers, investors, suppliers, and employees share common needs and benefit from working to ensure the success of everyone in the ecosystem.

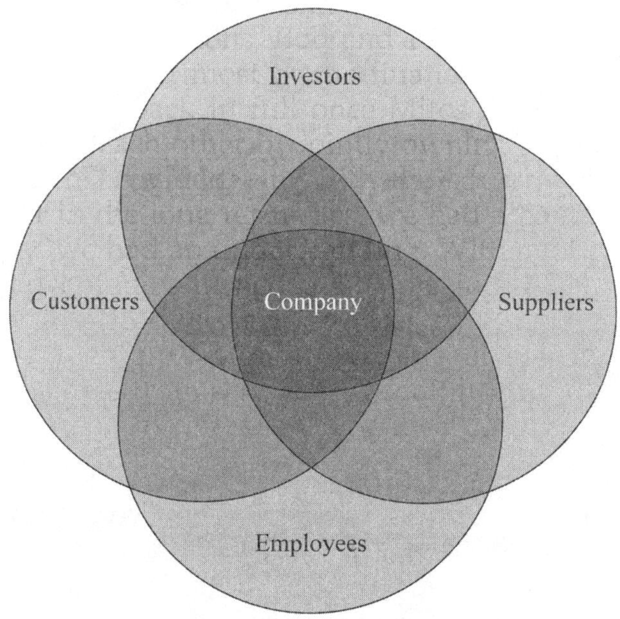

This view requires a long-term approach and a true understanding of constructive self-interest. If decisions are based solely on the short term, a company will try to take advantage of its customers whenever possible. This may benefit the business today, but it creates a customer who will search for a new supplier. While a company may vigorously haggle with its suppliers to the point where they (the suppliers) can hardly make a profit, the company will find that either the suppliers will become too weak to provide value to the business or will choose to use their resources to help another customer (who may be the company's competitor).

Imitation Is the Sincerest Form of Flattery

When big companies subdivide themselves into smaller independent business units that are more closely linked to their ecosystem, they stand a far greater chance of mimicking the approaches that are so successful in smaller companies. This requires a culture of respect and leadership that delegates power to meaningful business units that are close enough to the customers and suppliers to ensure that knowledgeable decisions are made and strong, mutually beneficial relationships developed along the value chain. This type of structure will be more attractive to those with the entrepreneurial skills that companies so desperately need.

At the 2009 Wharton Entrepreneur Conference at the University of Pennsylvania, I was involved in a panel discussion titled "Entrepreneurship in Times of Economic Crisis." The first question a member of the audience asked was: "Is there any advantage to starting a business in a recession?" After I answered the question, laying out the arguments presented in this book, panel member Prasad Thammineni, a serial entrepreneur who is currently CEO of Pixily (an interactive document-management service), slyly mentioned that he was gaining on his large competitors because many of them had cut staff to the point that there was no one left in customer service to answer the phones. While I am sure that his competitors' shareholders are happy about this quarter's earnings, what about next year's numbers?

Entrepreneurs, do not fear Goliath; instead, understand him, and see and exploit his weakness. He has more to fear from you than you do from him.

What you should know:

- *Small businesses enjoy many advantages, and these often offset advantages of scale. Do not fear competing with big multinationals; instead, study and exploit their weaknesses.*

- *Large companies need to organize around their smallest identifiable business unit in order to achieve the focus and market orientation of small businesses. The closer the decision-making process is situated to the customer, the better the results.*

- *Building systems and processes that align employee self-interest with the long- term interests of your business and its stakeholders is key to organizational success.*
- *Value creation is optimized by valuing all parties in the ecosystem.*

Fifteen

The Early Stage of Early Stage

Enterprising young children often open lemonade stands in their neighborhoods. When Seth Priebatsch was fourteen years old, he took the lemonade stand concept and elevated it to a completely different level. Seth and a friend began their business venture by converting an old wagon into a mobile stand and stocked it with snacks and drinks. They embedded a mini-refrigerator in the wagon to keep the drinks nice and cold during the hot Boston summer days. Then, instead of limiting sales to their immediate neighborhood, Seth and his buddy decided to apply for a vendor's permit in the highly-trafficked area of Newbury Street in Boston. There were only twenty permits granted that year, but through a series of what he terms "half permissions," Seth eventually managed to garner all the signatures needed to obtain a permit. (Youth and determination have their privileges.)

Permit in hand, Seth and his friend journeyed to Newbury Street, lugging their cart along. The device was so old and shoddy that it couldn't move when burdened with the food and drinks, so Seth and his friend had to wheel the cart two blocks, run back and pick up the food and drinks, and then carry the products to the awaiting cart. Every morning, they repeated this Three-Stooges-like process for two long miles. Once they arrived on crowded Newbury Street, they spent the day successfully peddling food and cold drinks to local pedestrians.

Seth's parents took their children's educations very seriously, but their schooling was far from typical. In addition to schoolwork, the Priebatsch kids also learned practical business matters. Seth's mother had him balancing his own checkbook (which only had ten dollars in it) by the time he was six. When Seth was eight, his father began a routine of taking him and his sister to meet various business owners, ranging from biotech start-ups to car dealerships, so they could learn how businesses operated. Seth and his sister would quiz each owner, asking what they did, how they operated, and how they started in business. These visits made quite an impression on Seth and his sibling and provided them with a variety of experiences that they never forgot.

By the time he was a freshman in high school, Seth had made enough money from his food and drink cart venture to start a business called Giftopedia, an internet based e-commerce company where customers ordered gift items that were then mailed to a third party. Seth outsourced the development of Giftopedia to India, and every morning during his freshman and sophomore years of high school, he woke up at 5 a.m. to have a Skype teleconference with his overseas team. (On more than one occasion, he also landed in trouble with his teachers while conducting Skype conference calls to India during class time.) After two years of pouring everything he had—both emotionally and financially—into the business, Seth decided to close down the operation. Although he fervently wanted the project to succeed, he concluded that he simply did not understand the company's technology well enough to lead the team's programmers—a mistake he vowed to never repeat.

By his senior year of high school, Seth was on to his latest idea, Postcard Tech, which developed promotional CD-ROMs that were the size of a postcard. Their unique sizing enabled the CD-ROMs to be shipped based on the cost of a postcard (only seventeen cents), which provided tremendous savings for companies or organizations that used mass mailings. At age eighteen, he was able to outsource the manufacturing of the product to Hong Kong. Postcard Tech was and still is a success.

Even before Seth entered Princeton in 2007, he had spent time brainstorming with dozens of business owners, and he had already started four different businesses. While some of his ideas proved unsuccessful, they all provided valuable lessons and were part of Seth's deliberate practice to become a successful entrepreneur. Each venture raised the bar and was slightly more ambitious than the last. Fail or succeed, Seth's knowledge and passion for business intensified with every endeavor he tackled.

DreamIt Ventures Is Born

After selling Mitos in the summer of 2007, I needed a new direction in my life. I knew I could not sit around all day; I was far too restless and curious for an idle lifestyle. After some intense soul searching, I realized that what made me most proud about Mitos was that it had created a valuable product, provided individuals with good jobs and outstanding benefits, and evolved into a company where people truly enjoyed coming to work. Although I definitely benefited from Mitos financially, I also profited from it on an emotional level because it made a positive contribution to the world.

After contemplating my next goal in life, I realized how much I enjoyed pinpointing a need in the marketplace and building a solution for that need. Because of this, I recognized that, post-Mitos, I should concentrate on working in early-stage businesses.

In the fall of 2007, I began to investigate the idea of forming an early-stage venture fund to help very new businesses. My model was not much different than other venture capital (VC) firms, except that I focused on *very* early-stage ideas. In other words, I was interested in ideas at stages before an angel investor or a venture capitalist would even consider looking at the deal. I discussed my idea with lawyer Stephen Goodman, who then introduced me to two men: David Bookspan and Michael Levinson.

David Bookspan was a fifty-something attorney-turned-entrepreneur who co-founded and was president and CEO of MarketSpan, Inc. MarketSpan created an innovative service that aggregated and enhanced court docket information and created new marketing opportunities for legal professionals. The product brought undeniable value to the legal profession. MarketSpan was acquired and is now part of LexisNexis under the brand LexisNexis CourtLink. David possessed a youthful enthusiasm and loved a good challenge, and I immediately knew that we would have fun working together.

Michael Levinson was a serial entrepreneur who had followed a career path similar to mine, co-founding PTS Learning Systems when he was in his midtwenties. PTS focused on corporate computer training and electronic performance support tools and software. Michael grew the company into a highly-profitable international organization prior to selling it in 1999. Michael was my polar opposite—a strong operations person with an unmatched attention to detail. I knew that we would make a great team.

For several years, David and Michael had bounced around various ideas to help early-stage businesses. Nothing much came of their brainstorming until the summer of 2007 when they started to learn more about a new type of Venture Capital firm called Y Combinator that was emerging on the West Coast.

Filling a Gap in the Market

As discussed throughout this book, the greatest opportunities often lie in quickly-evolving markets, and after meeting with David and Michael, I became convinced that early-stage investing was one of these markets. The cost of developing a business from scratch has been decreasing for decades. Several macro trends support this. For example, in the software/Web arena, new tools dramatically speed up the time needed to build products. In the physical sciences, the ability to outsource manufacturing to other local suppliers and build complex prototypes of everything from plastic widgets to electronic components requires only a modest budget. Compared to previous eras, forming partnerships and scaling successful ideas can occur relatively quickly and inexpensively.

At the same time, important changes have occurred since the 2000 dot-com revolution:

1) VCs learned the hard way that if they were involved in too many deals, they were potentially unable to

properly monitor or support them. This led investors to minimize the number of deals in which they participated and work with only a handful of larger prospects.

2) Many of the most successful funds were investing farther downstream, after ideas had been derisked. Success breeds imitation, so eventually, most funds moved downstream.

3) Successful VCs went on to raise large sums of money in subsequent funds and therefore had too much money to spend on small deals. Unsuccessful funds disappeared, leaving few in the early-stage investing arena.

While all of this occurred, angel investors followed venture capitalists upstream to support more mature deals. This left very few people interested in investing in pre-revenue businesses from first-time entrepreneurs. It left a gap that David, Michael, and I wanted to fill.

The convergence of these trends for new businesses created a new need in the marketplace. So when David and Michael pitched the idea of DreamIt (www.dreamitventures.com) to me, my immediate reply was: "How do I join your team?"

Essentially, DreamIt is a Darwinist approach to early stage investing, designed to either catapult a business forward or determine if it should die quickly and relatively cost-effectively. Here's how DreamIt helps businesses determine into which category they fall:

- **Money.** If I ask entrepreneurs with an idea what they need to succeed, most of them have a one-word reply: funding. While I do not think funding is necessarily *the* most critical element of a company's success, I will concede that entrepreneurs need money to survive while they are building their dream. At DreamIt, we provide adequate funding to enable people to survive while focusing on their idea.

- **Collaborative Atmosphere**. As mentioned earlier, it is critical in the early stage of a business to perfect the concept by discussing it with others. The idea behind

DreamIt is to fund ten to fifteen companies at a time and provide an open workspace in which people can easily bounce suggestions off one another, as well as dissect their ideas and share technological expertise. Together, participants provide each other with a support system that is essential in battling the challenges of early stage business.

- **Mentorship**. I was lucky enough to have strong mentors guide me through my journey at Mitos. At DreamIt, we developed a pool of experienced, creative mentors who we link to different companies that we fund. The mentors share a percentage of ownership in the DreamIt fund and therefore have a vested interest in helping the company succeed.

- **Donated Legal and Accounting Assistance.** Lawyers may prove expensive for young entrepreneurs, yet they definitely are needed in early stage businesses. At DreamIt, some of the region's top firms donate their time in an effort to help start-ups properly establish themselves, protect their intellectual property, and handle various legal issues. Receiving legal advice from top law firms helps businesses position themselves for the next round of funding, if necessary. As mentioned, anything that eliminates risk increases the value of a business. There are so many examples of investors being burned by early stage businesses with incomplete or incorrect corporate documents that an association with a well-established law firm is critical to a new company's fundraising. This same thought process holds true when early businesses are supported by experienced accountants—properly establishing finances from the start decreases the risk for future investors.

- **Rounding Out a Team**. Some people have creative ideas but do not possess the business or technical skills to turn their idea into a reality. At DreamIt, we gather individuals with the necessary resources needed to build excellent teams and businesses. We have what we call a strategist track, which allows people with a strong business background to apply to join a business that has a great concept. We also have what we call a hacker track, in which programmers and coders apply to join teams that may not have the technical ability to build their product.

- **Demo Day**. The culmination of DreamIt Ventures is a Demo Day, during which each DreamIt company presents its product or business to angel investors and venture capitalists in an effort to raise money (if it is required).

DreamIt Ventures was created as a preseed venture fund to nurture enthusiastic, bright, and motivated people with big ideas who can build a prototype, beta, or market-ready product or service within three months. By providing the tools needed to flourish, this new model for funding simultaneously accelerates the development of new businesses and increases their likelihood of success.

In essence, DreamIt allows start-up companies to progress by eliminating as many risks as possible. For some participants who enter the program with just an idea, the three months is used to develop the product and eliminate the risk of building it. For companies with an early stage product, the time period allows them to test, understand, and refine its value to potential customers.

Helping Entrepreneurs Soar

When Seth Priebatsch applied to DreamIt, the eighteen-year-old had completed half of his freshman year at Princeton. His company, Postcard Tech, was progressing well, but ready for a new and bigger challenge. Seth developed a concept for using cell phones to play in an interactive scavenger hunt. Determined not to repeat his mistakes of the past, he immersed himself in the mobile phone technology market and quickly (and without spending any money) determined that his concept could become a reality, at least from a technical standpoint. He began to share his idea with others to gather feedback and refine the concept. He simultaneously started building a team, a prototype, and a business plan. Seth Priebatsch applied to

DreamIt with his idea. In Seth, we saw a brilliant young entrepreneur with a solid idea, excellent technical skills, and the makings of a team.

Seth's idea was ambitious, and both he and the team at DreamIt realized that to penetrate the market quickly he needed additional resources. DreamIt introduced Seth to Michael Hagan, a strategist who had applied to DreamIt.

Michael was just a few years older than Seth. A Philadelphia native, Michael had cofounded collegeweb.com, a social networking site in the pre-Facebook days. While Michael and his team raised funding and built a solid product, they were simply beaten to the punch—and ultimately lost business to—Facebook. Demonstrating resilience, Michael accepted the defeat as part of his learning process, moved on, and looked for his next business opportunity. Michael Hagan applied to DreamIt as a strategist. In Michael, we saw an experienced entrepreneur who in many ways had learned the hard lessons of creating an early stage start-up. Michael had some technical skills, but his strengths were in sales and strategic planning.

Allow Me to Introduce You ...

After Seth had been accepted into DreamIt in the spring of 2008, DreamIt served as the venue for Seth and Michael's introduction. It proved a good fit. Seth provided Michael with an opportunity to earn an equity stake in his company, and, in exchange, he received an experienced, motivated, and focused strategist who woke up every day thinking about how to turn SCVNGR (www.scvngr.mobi) into a success.

With DreamIt's funding, an office, Chris Stanchak (founder of TicketLeap) as his mentor, Wolfe Block as his law firm, Parente Randolph as his accounting firm, and Michael Hagan as his strategist, Seth had the tools needed to propel his idea forward. Within five months, this incredible team had a product that was being used by tens of thousands of people and generating significant revenue. While Seth, Michael, and the rest of the team built this business, DreamIt provided the framework to catapult it forward, refine the value of the product, and demonstrate market acceptance.

Though the company could have rapidly reached a positive cash-flow position, Seth and his team decided to raise money in hopes of growing the business more quickly. Six months after entering the DreamIt program, SCVNGR raised money from Highland Capital and was well on its way to developing a strong, enduring business.

On a Mission

Our mission at DreamIt is to provide a unique set of resources that allow early stage businesses to increase their likelihood of success or to fail as quickly and capital efficiently as possible. Like all businesses, we will continue to refine our process to ensure that we provide the greatest value; however, we are positioned to meet our mission.

Investing in early stage businesses is not only critical for regions, but for society as a whole. I realize that this sounds a bit lofty, but I firmly believe that start-ups provide the innovation and creativity to invent products and services that positively impact the world and are critical to our evolution as a well-functioning society. Unfortunately, the market is moving to invest in only a handful of early stage start-ups, and with fewer companies entering the top business funnel, fewer will fall out of the bottom of the funnel. As a country, we must find ways to reverse this trend.

What you should know:

- *Small entrepreneurial projects are critical to the learning process for any aspiring entrepreneur.*
- *Treating failure as part of the learning process is a must for successful entrepreneurs.*
- *Entrepreneurship can be difficult and risky; DreamIt helps to minimize both factors.*

Sixteen

The Entrepreneurial Bond

More than a dozen successful entrepreneurs have been profiled throughout this book. While each of their amazing stories is unique, they all share a few powerful similarities.

The Common Threads Among Entrepreneurs

Every entrepreneur I interviewed was clearly impacted and uplifted by supportive family members and role models. For example, Dave Willis' father always said: "When you own your own business" as if to embed entrepreneurship into his son at a young age, and Albert Charpentier's wife encouraged him by stating: "If you are going to work so hard, you may as well work hard for yourself." Encouragement from loved ones reinforced the entrepreneurs' spirits when business challenges seemed insurmountable.

All of the entrepreneurs mentioned also have a passion for what they do. Just look at Don Long, who is in his seventies and spent thirty years building his company, yet still helps his sons nurture the family business, Integra. Or look at Don Katz, who experienced an incredible roller-coaster ride during his fourteen years as a business owner, yet remains as energized about the company as he was on day one.

Each of these entrepreneurs faced a failure or two, yet every one of them marched on, acknowledging failure as a necessary element of the learning process—whether it was fifteen-year-old Seth Priebatsch who learned the hard way to ensure that he understood the technological aspects of launching his product, or Blake Jennelle, who discovered during his first business venture that to succeed, he had to provide customers with what they needed, not necessarily what was "cool."

All of these people succeeded in their venture, yet each time they met their goals, they advanced even further, be it David Bookspan, who developed and sold MarketSpan, but returned with higher goals to cofound Monetate, or Ken Baker, who continues to grow NewAge and is determined to take his business to the next level.

The Differences Among Entrepreneurial Paths

Although they all share some of the same traits, each of the entrepreneurs triumphed in distinctive surroundings and circumstances. Seth Priebatsch dropped out of college after his freshman year to start SCVNGR, while David Bookspan left a lucrative law practice in his forties to start a technology business.

Albert Charpentier set out on an incredibly ambitious path to build the very first multimedia computer, while Alfred Baker built a simple distribution business.

Eric Bezos raised millions of dollars in venture capital and took his company public, while Mark Baiada reached a half-billion dollars in revenue without ever taking a dime from any investors.

Bill Gore was a visionary who not only developed a valuable product, but created a revolutionary type of company culture.

Three of the business owners were forced into the process, including Don Long who lost his job and became an entrepreneur in order to feed his four children.

Some companies like Audible took a decade to reach profitability, while others, like Mike Levinson and PTS Learning, reached profitability almost from day one.

Some of these entrepreneurs were incredible salespeople, like Dave Willis who after being fired from his previous job went on to surpass the amount of sales reached by his former employer within two years.

Others were natural technologists, like Bob Elbich who loved digging into detailed designs.

Alfred Baker started NewAge on his own; David Bookspan started both CourtLink and Monetate with a partner who had complementary skills.

The differences between these entrepreneurs are vast, yet they have more to do with the types of businesses they founded and the paths that each person chose.

All Together Now ...

The similarities in these entrepreneurs, however, are core to what shaped each one of them. The support they received as youngsters and throughout their lives provided them with the tools and the encouragement to take risks and learn from their mistakes. This allowed them to turn their inherent traits into the skills that allowed them to select the path that made sense, based on their own situation. This support, coupled with the purpose that they found in entrepreneurship, created a passion that ultimately allowed them to build success on the backs of their failure and, most importantly, to build more success on top of their initial success. While their personalities and their businesses vary, these entrepreneurs all share common characteristics that inspire them to achieve.

Seventeen

It's a Crazy Adventure

I don't like heights, but in the summer of 2003, I decided to go skydiving. I'm not sure why I chose to leap from a plane into the sky, but for some reason, it just seemed like the right time to try it. My good friend Kim also wanted to skydive, so the two of us trekked up the New Jersey turnpike to Jersey Shore Skydiving Adventures.

Although I have known her for years, I didn't realize it until we arrived at Skydiving Adventures that Kim and I have polar opposite views on life. She believes that each person's destiny is set and that everything happens for a reason. As you may have deduced from your reading thus far, I believe that we also play a role in determining our own fate. While there certainly are events that take place that are out of our control, we must also take advantage of the challenges presented to us in setting our own course in life. So as you can imagine, with two totally different mind-sets, Kim and I approached our skydiving outing quite differently. After taking an instruction course, we received our equipment and were ready to go. From that point on, Kim did not ask any questions; she simply hopped into the plane and said, "Let's go!" I, on the other hand, wanted to know who packed the chute and asked for a signed-off checklist to ensure that everything had been processed properly. When the skydiving instructors informed me that no such checklist existed, my high anxiety shot threw the roof. I remember saying to the instructor, "Are you *crazy*? What do you mean, you don't know who packed the chute?" But he just laughed it off and said, "That's just the way we do it."

The plane that took divers up in the air was a Cessna 172 that only held four people. Since Kim and I had decided to film the experience, only one of us could jump at a time to make room for the cameraperson. After learning about the Center's safety techniques (or lack thereof), I felt nauseous and was more than willing to let Kim go first.

For more than thirty minutes, I waited anxiously, searching the skies for Kim to come flying out. I grew more nervous by the second. Finally, I saw a small dot leave the plane almost 10,000 feet above me; it was Kim, with the instructor strapped to her back, hurling toward the earth. As I watched them free-falling, I decided that skydiving was definitely not for me and prayed that Kim's chute would open. Fortunately, all went well, and she landed gently on the ground, jubilant.

To Jump or Not to Jump ...

I can't often be talked into doing something that I have determined is not a good idea, but somehow Kim and the instructor managed to convince me to board the plane that day. While we ascended 10,000 feet, I could only think about the stupidity of this venture. Sitting in the plane, I did a quick risk-versus-reward calculation in my head and concluded that the reward seemed miniscule versus the risk of serious injury or death. While I was busy calculating my impending demise, my instructor and the cameraperson decided to have some fun with me. Just as we moved to the plane's open door, the cameraperson pointed at me and cried out to the instructor: "You forgot to strap him on." The instructor laughingly said "Oh, right" and acted as if he had just remembered to attach me to his back. At this point, my fear overpowered any sense of humor I had, and I think my instructor sensed it. After a brief and heated discussion, he assured me that we would not jump without my full consent and that he would not force me to leave the plane.

I stood at the edge of the aircraft with my knees knocking, staring down at the earth, far, far below. To this day I cannot tell you why, but I jumped. With my instructor on my back, we began tumbling toward the earth at 150 mph. I don't know exactly how long the free fall lasted, but it *seemed* like hours. The entire time, I simply prayed for the chute to open. When my instructor told me he was about to pull the chute, I was thrilled that the moment of truth was upon us. When the chute mercifully opened, a sense of relief flooded over me, and I actually enjoyed the rest of the ride.

What Does Logic Have to Do With It?

No logical, rational person will jump out of an airplane—or start a business. Both require either a confidence in the unknown or in one's self that is not only irrational, but borderline insane. Every new business comes so loaded with risk that no reasonable person would pursue it. Perhaps the most difficult challenge that entrepreneurs face is listening with an open mind to others' advice while developing the confidence to move forward in what appears to be a very risky proposition.

If you decide to pursue your entrepreneurial idea, in the beginning, formative stages of the business, you will probably work more hours for less pay than any job you have ever had and change course several times. You may have days when you are on top of the world and sure that nothing can stop your business from succeeding, followed by other days where you pray that a check arrives so that you can make payroll.

Remember, you are your greatest resource. Use your time wisely. Develop your core assumptions, and prove their accuracy. Adjust if necessary. Focus on where your product or service brings value. Think outside the box; nontraditional financing is available for good ideas. Surround yourself with people who possess complementary skills. Build a culture that is rooted in respect from day one. Communicate your purpose to everyone around you. Find or create a supportive network.

We all have the traits needed to succeed as entrepreneurs; years of societal evolution have ensured this. Find your passion, and ensure that you develop means of transitioning your inherited traits into the skills required for success.

No Time Like the First Time

Looking back on my skydiving experience, I wish that I had been relaxed enough during the entire free fall to fully enjoy the ride. Although there is no "rush" quite like skydiving, I will never do it again. I can say the same about my journey at Mitos. The parachute has opened, and I am now enjoying the safe ride back down to earth, but I will never take this exact path again, and I wish I had spent more time enjoying the early years of my business. While I don't regret the work that I put into Mitos, I wish that I could have more fully savored the successes and failures that we experienced along the way. To entrepreneurs, there is nothing like their first project. Much like a skydive, it creates a free fall that will either end in success or failure. Once you jump, you will move at 150 mph, with hair streaming back, screaming at the top of your lungs. People on earth will view you as a small dot, watching you with excitement as you grow bigger and bigger, admiring your courage, yet fearing for your life. I am confident that I will be successful at other ventures, but starting a business from scratch in my twenties with hardly a dime to my name and little experience is something I will never be able to replicate.

I encourage others to take the entrepreneurial jump and to thoroughly relish the entire excursion. Once the parachute is open, it is still an enjoyable ride, but there is simply nothing like the free fall.

Epilogue

On the morning of September 11, 2001, I was sharing a 10′ × 10′ office with Mitos' first two employees when someone rushed in to tell us that one of the World Trade Centers had been struck by an airplane. The three of us immediately rushed over to a neighboring office to follow the coverage on TV. I regret to say that I watched the second plane strike the second tower on live television. As the tragedy unfolded, I numbly called my good friend, David Suarez, who was working as a consultant on the ninety-ninth floor of the North Tower. None of my calls went through, so I frantically tried to e-mail him, but again, there was no response.

At noon, I closed the office at Mitos and drove to my parents' house. Later that afternoon, my father and I decided to escape the madness by going sailing on the Chesapeake Bay. There was not a boat in the water or a plane in the sky. It was eerily peaceful, yet that afternoon marked the beginning of a different world for me and for many others of my generation who considered war as a distant image that occurred only in foreign lands.

David did not return my call or respond to my e-mail. His body was not recovered until the spring of 2002. You'll remember that I roomed with David for two years during our college days. He was my cohort in our carpet-selling business. More than any other person I have known, he looked for the positive aspect in the people and the world around him. *The New York Times* wrote the following story about twenty-four-year-old David:

> *David Suarez cared. He cared about people who did not have his opportunities, people who did not have his education, people who had to struggle. "He reached out to people in a very warm and genuine way," said Ted Suarez, his father. "Everyone remembered his smile. From a little boy, he had a smile that was very endearing."*
>
> *Mr. Suarez, 24, was a systems consultant who worked for Deloitte Consulting. He reported each day to the office of*

> *his client, Marsh & McLennan, in the World Trade Center. He was in the process of sending out applications to colleges, because next fall he wanted to embark on an M.B.A. before returning to Deloitte. His hope was to go to Harvard.*
>
> *But he always made time for the needy. Social concern was a family tradition. He volunteered for the nonprofit group New York Cares. He worked in soup kitchens and tutored high school students for their college entrance exams.*
>
> *He always gave the disadvantaged the benefit of the doubt. Friends told a story about how they found him once talking to some beggars outside a bar. Mr. Suarez asked one of the beggars, who was in a wheelchair, "What would it take to make you happy?"*
>
> *The man said, "Give me $20."*
>
> *Mr. Suarez gave him $20.*
>
> *The beggar got up, folded up his wheelchair and walked off.*
>
> *Mr. Suarez was not angry. The episode did not make him jaded. He shrugged it off. By his thinking, he would rather lose $20 here and there to an impostor than risk spurning someone who really needed his help. He kept on giving.* [14]

I was not with David when he gave away the $20, but that incident serves as a perfect example of his character. You could turn to him when you needed a positive outlook or a word of encouragement. During my years at Penn State, David was the one with whom I could debate the topics of the day and share my crazy concepts. On occasion, I was actually able to convince him that my ideas were worth pursuing. David was a young man, just starting out his life in New York, yet hundred of mourners flocked to his funeral. As so often is true of great people such as David, I selfishly thought I was the only one that had a unique relationship with him. But in reality his magnetic personality drew people to him and provided each of them with a feeling of special friendship.

---

[14] Howell Raines and Janny Scott, Portraits 9/11/01: the collected "Portraits of grief" from The New York times (Macmillian Press, 2002), 583.

David's father presented the following eulogy that I (and I suspect many others who were there) reflect upon on a daily basis.

"There is much I could say about David. You probably already know that he was an Eagle Scout, that he graduated from Penn State, and that he was a great employee. But that is not what made him special to us. What made him special is that he valued relationships far more than material achievement and was not willing to gain the world at the expense of his soul. After reading the stories that many of you have written about David, there is very little that I could say that you do not already know. I will, therefore, ask you to close your eyes to listen to my words and your own thoughts about him. To see his big smile, to remember his zest for life, and in particular to recall an event you experienced with him. I will ask you to dream. Yes, to dream of what our lives can be like having known him. I will further ask you to commit to one action, which only you will know. For if we convert his and our dreams into action, he will live on through us to influence others and thus, his life will continue to have meaning.

"In his writings (for his MBA application) here is how he described the start of a normal workday: 'The subway pulls into the Fulton Street station. I look up from the *New York Times,* grab my bag and join the migration toward the World Trade Center. The Marsh project is at an interesting point. I settle into my desk on the 99th floor, to the backdrop of the Brooklyn Bridge and the morning sun hovering over the distant Long Island. I start the day by reviewing the goal list I created last night. I look up, the sun has risen slightly and people have begun to trickle in. Ahhh … I am ready to begin.'

"And ready he was, for it was on a day such as he described, that he took his first step into eternity.

"David, we all are running the race to arrive where you are. As a runner, you never were one to wait around. You got there first. We mourn your departure but rejoice at your arrival. With the grace of God we will see you some day. To paraphrase from Ted Kennedy's address memorializing his bother Robert: Most of us dream dreams and ask why? David, you would ask, why not? and then proceed to make them happen. We must now make his dreams and our dreams come true."

I did make a commitment that day. I committed to a dream that David and I shared: leaving the world a better place than we found it. This is my purpose.

I often find myself wishing that David had woken up fifteen minutes late that morning or missed the train so that I would still be able to debate the issues of the day with my good friend. But as is so often true in life, it is the small things that make an enormous difference, and there is a certain randomness to the world around us. David's story taught me not only these facts, but how short and precious life can be.

We all have a role to play in society. I am not a physician or a politician. Like so many other people, I was born an entrepreneur and found purpose in it. With the help of many others, I have been able to keep the entrepreneur in me alive and convert my inherited traits into the skills needed to succeed. I am fortunate to be able to give back to the world by helping it operate more efficiently, thus creating good jobs and increasing the quality of life for employees.

This is the difference that I can make.

I hope that this book provides guidance for you to do the same.